D0146343

R. Henry Migliore
Robert E. Stevens
David L. Loudon
Stan Williamson

Strategic Planning for Not-for-Profit Organizations

The Haworth Press, Inc.

Strategic Planning for Not-for-Profit Organizations

HAWORTH Marketing Resources
Innovations in Practice & Professional Services
William J. Winston, Senior Editor

Strategic Planning for Not-for-Profit Organizations

R. Henry Migliore, PhD
Robert E. Stevens, PhD
David L. Loudon, PhD
Stan Williamson, PhD

The Haworth Press
New York • London • Norwood (Australia)

The Haworth Press, Inc., 10 Alice Street, Binghamton, NY 13904-1580

Library of Congress Cataloging-in-Publication Data

Strategic planning for not-for-profit organizations / R. Henry Migliore . . . [et al.].
     p.   cm. – (Haworth marketing resources)
    Includes bibliographical references and index.
    ISBN 1-56024-919-6.
    1. Nonprofit organizations–Management. 2. Strategic planning. I. Migliore, R. Henry. II. Series.
HD62.6.S765 1994
658.4′012–dc20
                                                              94-10900
                                                                   CIP

CONTENTS

ABOUT THE AUTHORS

R. Henry Migliore, PhD, is Professor of Strategic Planning and Management at Northeastern University/University Center at Tulsa where he teaches both graduate and undergraduate courses. He was formerly Dean of the ORU School of Business and a Visiting Professor at the University of Calgary. Dr. Migliore is the author of numerous articles and books on planning and management and has worked with many nonprofit organizations in developing strategic plans.

Robert E. Stevens, PhD, is Professor of Marketing in the College of Business Administration at Northeast Louisiana University in Monroe, Louisiana. He has served as a consultant to local, regional, and national firms for research projects, feasibility studies, and marketing planning, and has been a partner in a marketing research company. Dr. Stevens is the author of 11 books and more than 80 articles on management, finance, and marketing.

David L. Loudon, PhD, is Professor of Marketing and Head of the Department of Management and Marketing in the College of Business Administration at Northeast Louisiana University. Dr. Loudon is the author of books on consumer behavior, marketing planning, and church marketing, as well as numerous articles. He has served as a consultant to various organizations and is president of a computer software firm.

Stan Williamson, PhD, is Assistant Professor of Management at Northeast Louisiana University. He teaches strategy, human resource management, and management principles. Previously, he served as a senior executive for a regional health care system for 13 years and as a consultant in the health care field.

Preface

Three primary considerations were used in preparing the book. The first was length. We wanted to keep the amount of reading material brief enough to be read and reviewed quickly. Therefore, only essential concepts and techniques are presented in a very concise form.

The second consideration was to present material that was theoretically sound but practically oriented. We wanted the reader to be able to put the concepts presented to immediate use in decision making. We have also included worksheets at the end of each chapter to help readers develop their own strategic plans.

The final consideration was to provide a thorough set of appendixes to illustrate various aspects of strategic planning and sample strategic plans. Thus the reader will not only read about strategic planning, but actually see what a strategic plan looks like. This is useful in evaluating plans prepared by others or in preparing your own.

The end result, we believe, is a book which is both readable and helpful to those involved with the administration of not-for-profit organizations. We hope the book will serve as both a tutorial and an easily accessible reference for readers.

Acknowledgements

A book is seldom the work of the authors alone but involves the efforts of a great number of people. We would specifically like to thank the following people for their contributions: Melinda Calhoun who tirelessly typed the final versions of the manuscript; Melissa Hewlett and Sherry Stewart, graduate students in the MBA program at Northeast Louisiana University, for their research assistance; and finally, the administration of Northeast Louisiana University for their support of this project.

Chapter 1

Planning Perspectives

You've got to come up with a plan. You can't wish things will get better.

John F. Welch
CEO, General Electric

As the environment of not-for-profits becomes increasingly dynamic, strategic management becomes more and more important.

Peter Wright
Professor of Strategic Management

. . . nonprofits need management even more than business does, precisely because they lack the discipline of the bottom line.

Peter Drucker
Management Expert

Commitment isn't enough anymore. You also have to have professionalism, or you're going to go out of business.

John R. Garrison
President, National Easter Seal Society

In the most successful not-for-profits, the attitude is entrepreneurial and the approach is strictly businesslike.

Edward Skloot
Management Consultant

If you are struggling with any of the following problems or questions, this book may be very important to you:

- Why is there so much confusion among our assistant directors on what we are trying to accomplish?
- Why is there so much dissension and disagreement in this organization?
- Why is there such a high turnover of people in our organization, especially in leadership positions?
- Why did we spend money on new services when they are not being used?
- As an administrator, why am I working 12 hours a day, and can never keep up?
- Why have we failed on a number of projects and programs?
- Why has our funding dropped off?
- Why does this organization lack enthusiasm?
- Why has the board asked me to resign after everything I have put into this organization?

If you are wrestling with any of these questions, the answer might be that your not-for-profit (NFP) organization lacks good long-term strategic planning. And you would be in good company. Consider the recent sagas of such diverse organizations as the Boy Scouts of America (BSA), Springmaid Federal Credit Union, and the Ford Foundation. What do these organizations have in common? They all are not-for-profit firms that have faced up to and successfully overcome declining memberships or enrollments and serious revenue shortfalls.

Each of these organizations can attribute their new-found success to effective use of strategic plans. After systematic analysis, the BSA realized the world they sought to serve had changed, and they had not. Adapting to their potential membership's new interests by doing things like offering computer skill merit badges and by getting their story out to corporate sponsors, achieved a dramatic turnaround. Membership was the largest in 14 years and resulted in a $1 million profit.[1]

Similarly, Springmaid Federal Credit Union of Lancaster, South Carolina was struggling to survive. The local economy had been very weak during the 1970s, reflecting sluggish demand for textiles, the major employer in this rural area. As with the BSA, Springmaid realized it must effect a plan that better met the preferences of its membership if it was to survive. Based on a review of the opportunities and threats Springmaid faced in its environment and its own strengths and weaknesses, a strategic plan was developed. Membership requirements were redefined and extended to virtually all residents in its market area. New services such as checking accounts and automatic teller machines were offered, and six branch offices were opened. The results of this strategic management effort were dramatic. Springmaid began the 1980s with $38 million in assets, but finished the decade with assets of $231 million. Its membership grew from 18,457 in 1980 to 44,945 by 1989. With an effective strategic plan, you could say Springmaid found itself "laughing all the way to the credit union."[2]

The Ford Foundation made a similar move, turning around a dwindling endowment that had dropped from $4 billion in 1964 to $2.3 billion in 1979. The financial hemorrhaging was stinted after the president initiated a strategic audit of the foundation, identifying operational strengths and weaknesses. The review allowed expenses to be cut in line with the reduced level of endowment revenues. Strategic planning also identified new opportunities to engage in joint ventures with other organizations to increase grant making. The results: 1989 saw grants of $218 million distributed, well over the $84.6 million extended in 1979. All this, while the endowment increased to $5.6 billion with stock market improvements.[3]

In the past, traditional business enterprises were the primary users of strategic planning. Increasingly, however, not-for-profits have begun to apply strategic planning concepts to improve the effectiveness of their operations. And, as we shall see, a fundamental part of strategic planning is the team-building approach of developing leaders and involving people in the plan.

NOT-FOR-PROFIT ORGANIZATIONS

The typical profit-seeking firm relies almost solely on the sale of its goods or services to the public for its revenue. There are other organizations that are by their designation not-for-profit (or NFPs, as we will often refer to them), which differ fundamentally from the traditional proprietary business operation. Let's explore the differences.

Almost all organizations can be classified into four types.

1. Private for-profit firms. From Mom and Pop stores to global enterprises, these firms seek income by selling their goods or services in the marketplace.
2. Private not-for-profit organizations. These seek to serve the public also but may rely heavily on membership fees, endowments, donations, and contributions, in addition to revenue they may generate directly from the sale of their goods or services.
3. Private quasi-public organizations. These are government regulated monopolies, such as electrical utility companies, authorized by legislative act to provide specialized goods or services to particular populations.
4. Public governmental agencies. Funded by taxes and direct fees for services, these are created by law at the federal, state, and local levels to provide public services.

This book is designed specifically for not-for-profit organizations. Here, we intend the term not-for-profit to include the private not-for-profit organizations described above such as churches, private universities, health care organizations, arts organizations, and traditional charities. We also mean for it to include public governmental units like state colleges, law enforcement agencies, and drivers' license bureaus.

PLANNING IS IMPORTANT

Planning as part of the management process is crucial to the success of any organization. This is especially true for not-for-profit organizations. However, the increasing volatility of the environments in which all organizations, including not-for-profits, must function has forced major changes in the scope of the planning process. No longer will it suffice simply to lay plans for internal operations. To adapt to ever changing environmental forces, organizations have moved to strategic planning, with its greater emphasis on stretching the organization, to maintain a proper fit between it and the demands of its environment.

Out of a large number of decisions made by an organization or by an individual administrator, there are a handful of critical ones that can significantly impact the future of the organization or its leader. These strategic decisions require careful identification and thoughtful consideration. This is the nature of the role of strategic planning.

Perspectives of strategic thinking can be illustrated with this question: Who are the two most important persons responsible for the success of an airplane's flight? A typical response would be:

> the pilot and the navigator, or
> the pilot and the maintenance supervisor, or
> the pilot and the air traffic controller, or
> the pilot and the flight engineer.

All of these responses recognize the day-to-day hands-on importance of the pilot. They all introduce one of several other important support or auxiliary functionaries to the answer. However, each of these segmented responses ignores the one person who is perhaps the single most important individual to the ultimate success of the airplane–the designer. Perhaps the pilot and the designer are the two most important individuals to the success of an airplane. The pilot because of his day-to-day responsibilities in commanding the craft and the designer because of his ability to create a concept that can be economically constructed, easily operated by any normally competent flight crew, and maintained safely by the ground crew.

Most contemporary administrators of not-for-profits perceive themselves as the "pilot" of their organizations; taking off, landing, conferring with the navigator, and communicating with the air traffic controller. They generally view themselves as the chief hands-on operational managers. However, what has been most lacking in these organizations in the past few years has been an appreciation for the strategic viewpoint. There is a need for more emphasis on the "designer" approach to operating a not-for-profit venture. A well conceived strategic planning system can facilitate this emphasis.

A not-for-profit organization without a long-term planning perspective faces a tough situation. Instead of moving steadily toward its goals, the organization will continually swerve off course due to the endless supply of distractions that can prevent a not-for-profit from pursuing its purpose and vision. Thus, strategic planning is one of the keys to success of any undertaking, and nowhere is it more important than in not-for-profit organizations.

WHAT IS PLANNING?

Planning may be defined as a managerial activity which involves determining your fundamental purpose as an organization, analyzing the environment, setting objectives, deciding on specific actions needed to reach the objectives, and then adapting the original plan as feedback on results is received. This process should be distinguished from the plan itself, which is a written document containing the results of the planning process what is to be done and how it is to be done. Planning is a continuous process: which both precedes and follows other functions. Plans are made and executed, and results are used to make new plans as the process continues.

TYPES OF PLANS

There are many types of plans but most can be categorized as either *strategic* or *tactical.* Strategic plans cover a long period of time and may be referred to as *long-term.* They are broad in scope and basically answer the question of how an organization is to commit its resources over the next five to ten years. Strategic plans are altered on an infrequent basis to reflect changes in the environment or overall direction of the organization.

Tactical plans cover a short time period, usually a year or less. They are often referred to as *short-term* or *operational* plans. They specify what is to be done in a given year to move the organization toward its long-term objectives. In other words, what we do this year (short-term) needs to be tied to where we want to be five to ten years in the future (long-term).

Most not-for-profits which have been involved in planning have focused on short-term rather than long-term planning. This is better than not planning at all; but it also means each year's plan is not related to anything long-term in nature and usually falls short of moving the organization to where it wants to be in the future.

Programs and events require planning also. A *program* is a large set of activities involving a whole area of a not-for-profit's capabilities, such as planning for a new outpatient surgery program or a new symphony concert series. Planning for programs involves:

1. Dividing the total set of activities into meaningful parts.
2. Assigning planning responsibility for each part to appropriate people.
3. Assigning target dates for completion of plans.
4. Determining and allocating the resources needed for each part.

Each major program or division within a not-for-profit organization should have a strategic plan in place to provide a blueprint for the program over time.

An *event* is generally a project of less scope and complexity. It is also not likely to be repeated on a regular basis. An event may be a part of a broader program or it may be self-contained. Even when it is a one time event, planning is an essential element to accomplish the objectives of the project and coordinate the activities which make up the event. For example, a plan to have a fund raiser for the new symphony concert series would be an example of a project plan.

ADVANTAGES OF PLANNING FOR NOT-FOR-PROFIT ORGANIZATIONS

Why should a not-for-profit devote time to planning? Consider the following questions:

Do you know where you are going and how you are going to get there?

Does everyone in the organization know what you are trying to accomplish?

Does everyone in the organization know what is expected of them?

If the answer to any of these is no, then your not-for-profit needs to develop a long-range plan with as many people involved as possible. And it has never been more crucial in the dynamic environment your organization faces. Strategic planning can guide your organization through decision making and actions which determine whether an enterprise prospers, survives, or fails.

In many small not-for-profits, administrators may object to planning, thinking that it makes no sense for them; since they are only a small organization, everyone associated knows what happened in the past year and what is likely to happen in the coming year. Another objection often voiced is that there is no time for planning. A third objection is that there are not enough resources to allow for planning.

All these objections actually point out the necessity for planning even in the small not-for-profit. Such an organization may actually have a sizeable budget, making it imperative to have a plan of where the organization is heading. The feeling that there is no time for planning may seem accurate, but probably simply reflects the fact that the lack of planning in the past has left insufficient time for attention to such necessities. Finally, the argument that there are insufficient resources should justify the role of planning in order to obtain the maximum benefit from those resources being used in the organization. Thus, planning is a critical element in any not-for-profit's success.

Planning has many advantages. For example, it helps administrators adapt to changing environments, take advantage of opportunities created by change, reach agreements on major issues, and place responsibility more precisely. It also gives a sense of direction to staff members and provides a basis for gaining their commitment. The sense of vision that can be provided in a well written plan also instills a sense of loyalty in organization members or constituents.

A not-for-profit can benefit from the planning process because it is a systematic, continuing process that allows the NFP to:

1. Assess its market position. This involves what is termed a SWOT analysis–examining the not-for-profit's internal *S*trengths and *W*eaknesses and external *O*pportunities and *T*hreats. Without explicit planning these elements may go unrecognized.

2. Establish goals, objectives, priorities, and strategies to be completed within specified time periods. Planning will enable the not-for-profit to assess accomplishment of the goals that are set and will help motivate staff and volunteers to work together to achieve shared goals.
3. Achieve greater staff and member commitment and teamwork aimed at meeting challenges and solving problems presented by changing conditions.
4. Muster its resources to meet these changes through anticipation and preparation. "Adapt or die" is a very accurate admonition.

Administrators cannot control the future, but they should attempt to identify and isolate present actions and forecast how results can be expected to influence the future. The primary purpose of planning, then, is to see that current programs and findings can be used to increase the chances of achieving future objectives and goals; that is, to increase the chances of making better decisions today that affect tomorrow's performance.

Unless planning leads to improved performance, it is not worthwhile. Thus, to have a not-for-profit organization that looks forward to the future and tries to stay alive and prosperous in a changing environment, there must be active, vigorous, continuous, and creative planning. Otherwise, a not-for-profit will only react to its environment.

There are basically two reasons for planning: (1) protective benefits resulting from reduced chances for error in decision making and (2) positive benefits, in the form of increased success in reaching organizational objectives.

Some not-for-profits and their leaders who plan poorly, if at all, constantly devote their energies to solving problems that would not have existed, or at least would be much less serious, with planning. Thus they spend their time fighting fires rather than practicing fire prevention.

Long-range planning can become a means of renewal in the life of an organization if the following five significant points about planning are remembered:

1. A unified purpose can be achieved only when all segments of the not-for-profit organization see themselves as part of a larger whole with a single goal.
2. Isolated individual decisions and commitments often influence future plans, even when they are not intended to do so.
3. When careful planning is lacking, groups in the not-for-profit often become competitive with one another and duplicate one another's work.
4. Without coordinated planning, groups in the not-for-profit may come to feel they are ends in themselves and lose their sense of perspective in relation to the organization.
5. The magnitude of the tasks facing a not-for-profit demand long-range planning.[4]

PLANNING'S PLACE IN THE NOT-FOR-PROFIT ORGANIZATION

We are now ready to discuss who does the planning, or the place of planning in a not-for-profit organization. Obviously, all leaders engage in planning to some degree. As a general rule, the larger the not-for-profit organization becomes, the more the primary planning activities become associated with groups of people as opposed to individuals.

Many larger not-for-profits develop a planning committee or staff. Organizations set up such a planning team for one or more of the following reasons:

1. *Planning takes time.* A planning team can reduce the workload of individual staff or members.
2. *Planning takes coordination.* A planning team can help integrate and coordinate the planning activities of individual staff.
3. *Planning takes expertise.* A planning team can bring to a particular problem more tools and techniques than any single individual.
4. *Planning takes objectivity.* A planning team can take a broader view than one individual and go beyond specific projects and particular organizational departments.

A planning team generally has three basic areas of responsibility. First, it assists the administrator in developing goals, strategies, and policies for the organization. The planning group facilitates this process by scanning and monitoring the organization's environment. A second major responsibility of the planning team is to coordinate the planning of different levels and units within the not-for-profit. Finally, the planning group acts as an organizational resource for administrators who lack expertise in planning.

In smaller not-for-profits, planning and execution must usually be carried out by the same people. The greatest challenge is setting aside time for planning in the midst of all the other activities needed on a day-to-day basis.

RESISTANCE TO THE PLANNING PROCESS

There are three main reasons why planning does not get done in not-for-profit organizations today: (1) administrators lack training, (2) many perceive it as irrelevant, and (3) problems can occur in implementation.

Lack of Management Training

Many not-for-profit organizations are small, with an even smaller core of active members. The educational background and experience of the leaders of these organizations varies widely. Those with prior management experience often possess a proactive, can-do attitude and want to spend their time performing hands-on functions with which they are more comfortable. Furthermore, many not-for-profits cannot or do not draw on a pool of volunteers with management training or skills. For these reasons, the objective setting, strategy development, and other planning functions are largely neglected.

Planning Is Thought to Be Irrelevant

Developing objectives and strategies has been largely neglected or purposely avoided by many not-for-profits. This reluctance to plan stems from the fact that many view the application of strategic planning as irrelevant. Some have felt that because the environment in which not-for-profits work changes so rapidly, laying out formal plans and objectives is a useless endeavor.

With this view, constantly shifting environmental demands outside the not-for-profit's control can make objectives obsolete before they become official doctrine for the organization, so why develop them at all? Unfortunately, the consequence of this perspective is a leadership doomed to reactionary, piecemeal approaches to environmental demands, often resulting in less than desirable performance.

Other strategic goal-setting challenges in not-for-profits may color attitudes against planning. Many not-for-profits are service-oriented organizations. Services, unlike products, are intangible and often difficult to separate from the recipient of the service. This complicates specific goal setting and the measurement of results against the goals. In addition, not-for-profits often employ professionals to deliver their services. Professionals tend to be wed more to their profession and less to the organization and its objectives. This is particularly evident when, in the professionals' view, the organization's goals conflict with those of their profession.

Finally, not-for-profits face the daunting task of trying to serve the often varying interests of their members, service recipients, and funding sponsors. Some might say that setting official goals would serve only to please some constituencies while disaffecting others: better to be vague than risk losing participation and financial support.

Implementation Problems

Although there is much academic and theoretical support for planning, the actual implementation of it often runs aground on the shores of operational reality. Even among very progressive not-for-profits you find significant resistance to planning. Some of the most common arguments against it are:

1. Planning is not action-oriented.
2. Planning takes too much time; we are too busy to plan.
3. Planning becomes an end not just a means to an end.
4. Planning never ends up being carried out exactly as intended anyway.

Many of these arguments stem from the same kind of thinking that would say that the pilot was the most important person in the success of an airplane (referring back to the airplane/designer analogy). The feeling that planning is not "hands-on" and related to the important day-to-day operations of the not-for-profit is frequently heard. However, this point of view is shortsighted in terms of long-run success. Planning is not just for dreamers; in fact, it lets the not-for-profit's administrative team determine what can be done today to accomplish or avoid some future circumstance.

Planning sometimes becomes an end in the minds of some users. This is particularly true when it is established solely as a committee responsibility within an organization. A committee can facilitate the strategic planning process, but the process will not be a dynamic lifeblood activity of the organization without the ongoing involvement of the administrator and staff members.

President Dwight Eisenhower has been widely quoted as saying, "Plans are nothing, planning is everything." The truth he expressed was that the actual plan itself was not the end, but that the process of planning–developing futuristic scenarios, evaluating the environment and competition, assessing internal strengths and capabilities, revising objectives and tactics–as the organizational dialogue was most important. This dialogue ideally breaks down barriers to communication, exposes blind spots to the light, tests logic, measures the environment, and determines feasibility. The end result is more effective and efficient implementation of organizational activities.

Planning does not depend on complete forecasting accuracy to be useful. In sports even the very best game plans are often adapted as play goes on. Yet coaches continue to develop game plans with each new opponent. They understand that the importance of planning here is to keep your organization moving in the right direction even if the finer points of the plan are constantly being adjusted to new circumstances. And in making these adjustments, a variety of futuristic alternatives or scenarios can be very helpful in establishing planning parameters. Often a best-case, most-likely-case and worst-case approach is used. This three-level forecast gives dimension to the process of recognizing, anticipating, and "managing" change.

In spite of these and other perceived negatives, the advantages of planning far outweigh any disadvantages. Planning not only should be done but must be done.

REVENUE SOURCE INFLUENCES ON PLANNING

Executives of any business enterprise must be concerned about continuing, adequate sources of revenue for the survival of their business. Traditional businesses have a straightforward objective. They can focus on pleasing the customer. For the director of an NFP organization, however, these concerns are more complex.

For many not-for-profits, the focus on exactly who the customer is may become fuzzy. This is due to the fact that the recipient of an NFP's services may not be the same person who directly pays the bill. Medicare patients' hospital charges are paid directly by an intervening party, the federal government. United Way agencies' services are funded by donations from individuals and organizations which may never be recipients of the service. Public universities are largely funded by state legislatures.

Any organization–not-for-profit or proprietary–tends to concentrate on the desires of those who foot the bill. And to the extent that there is a funding sponsor providing financial support for the client, the client's influence over the NFP's goals and performance may be weakened.

One consequence of intervening sources of funding for NFPs is the tendency for NFPs to ignore the client's needs in favor of the funding sponsor's demands where the two conflict. In attempts to satisfy both parties, not-for-profit organizations may avoid goal setting or develop goals that are vague at best.

Unfortunately, highly generalized goals have their performance shortcomings. In contrast, there is plenty of evidence that goals which are relatively specific and measurable, wherever possible, support higher performance in organizations.

The message for not-for-profits is that the strategic planning process can provide the understandable goals they need. It does this by systematically considering the expectations of all those who hold a stake in the effectiveness of the NFP's operation. Thus strategic planning is the vehicle that can produce goals which are defined as clearly as possible toward the end of meeting both the client's needs and the scrutiny of the sponsor.

THE GREATEST NEEDS OF TODAY'S NOT-FOR-PROFIT ORGANIZATIONS

In informal surveys by the authors, leaders of not-for-profit organizations appear to be unanimous in their beliefs that strategic planning is important. Yet simple acknowledgement of its importance is not enough for success. To put matters into perspective, let us try to translate success for your NFP organization into a formula:

$$X = f(A,B,C,D,E,F,G,H,I \dots)$$

In this case X represents success, a dependent variable, and is on the left side of the equation. The = sign means a balance, or equal to what is on the other side; the f means "a function of," indicating on what that success depends. On the right side are all the independent variables that affect success:

A. Executive Director as Leader
B. Executive Director as Manager
C. Planning System
D. Organizational Structure
E. Control System
F. Needs of Constituencies Met
G. NFP's National Influence
H. NFP's Local Influence
 I. Location
   . . . etc.

Only a few independent variables are listed, but the possibilities are endless. Notice that success is not necessarily equated to size. We are defining success in broader terms than organizational membership, budget, and so forth. There seems to be a widespread notion that size is the only barometer of success, but we do not hold to that belief.

Untapped leadership exists in many NFPs. But we believe the

greatest problems holding back these leaders–and the organizations they serve–involve some combination of independent variables B, C, D, and E. Planning, organization, and control are some of the greatest needs of not-for-profits today.

We assume that all NFP administrators are to some degree leaders, or they could not remain in their executive positions. However, their leadership efforts and the success of their organizations are in direct proportion to variables B, C, D, and E. If you assume all other variables remain unchanged and full effort goes into B, C, D, and E, then the X factor (success), the dependent variable, has to increase. Without training and knowledge in the area of planning and management, your NFP has placed a ceiling on success. No organization can get any bigger than the capacity of its managers to manage. The hindrance is not the needs of the constituents, because they are always there. Nor is it the NFP's reputation or location; rather, it is simply planning, management, organization, and control.

If every NFP administrator could improve each of these areas just a little each year, they would be much more successful. They could reduce drastically all the obvious errors in direction, false starts, dissipated efforts, frustrated staff members, and waste. They could also successfully challenge a world rife with criticism about waste and inefficiency in NFPs.

Administrators cannot afford to wait until someone comes along and creates a big scandal about waste and inefficiency. We need to put our shoulders to the wheel and pay attention to planning, management, organization, control, and people. If we do not, on the whole, many of our not-for-profit organizations will not accomplish nearly as much as they are capable of.

Our observation is that many people in NFP leadership positions are reluctant to plan, do not want a plan in writing, and do not ask for advice. The tendency is to be led by intuition, which is sometimes based on a whim or emotional impulse. This reflects our general American inclination to "hang loose." Probably 75 percent of the profit-making organizations the authors have observed or worked with have the same problem. Yet the 25 percent that have the discipline to plan and manage properly far outperform those that do not. Higher profits, better service, lower turnover are but a few of the rewards. The same good fortune comes to those not-for-profits that have the discipline to plan and manage effectively.

Many times there is the tendency to say that forces outside our control caused a plan or project to go sour. And sometimes that is the case. But too often we are our own worst enemies, holding ourselves back. Many NFP failures can be traced to poor planning, failure to get people involved in the planning, and generally poor management.

Even where planning is done, we often sense a spirit of extreme urgency. Here the atmosphere is permeated with a "let's go for it–if it is a worthwhile service, it will prosper" mentality. What is the rush? Many NFP organizations need to slow down and plan. Often they have rushed around in circles for the past few years. If it is a worthwhile service, it deserves our best efforts at careful planning. Included in doing our best is using the best planning and management philosophies and techniques available.

Fundamental to these efforts is effective goal setting. Where planning in not-for-profits occurs without quantitative goals clearly understood and widely supported, vigorous progress is unlikely and probably impossible. The importance of goal setting is to provide direction and unity of purpose, but it must be the organization's goal, for it is not the planners but the organization that will ensure the plan's success. Planning is not easy but the alternative is for the organization to be tossed to and fro, buffeted by every unforeseen circumstance and blown off course.

And on a personal level, every leader needs a vision or a dream. Mission statements and dreams are the vessels through which personal desires can be fulfilled. Yet without specific goals, a vision is no vision.

In a society where many institutions are becoming stagnant, it is imperative that not-for-profits have an expanding vision. Thus, we see creative planning as the NFP's best hope for a successful future. Solid purpose, long-range dreaming, and visionary thinking should be basic to an NFP's operation. Too often planning in NFPs has been met with little enthusiasm. Even in larger not-for-profits, the enthusiasm for a plan seldom extends beyond a year unless it involves something tangible, like a new building. Yet no matter how misunderstood and poorly appreciated planning is, it is a major factor in effective NFP performance. The time for strategic planning in your not-for-profit is now.

SUMMARY

We have attempted to establish in this introduction our belief that: (1) methods used successfully in industry are applicable to not-for-profit organizations; (2) there is a place for better planning and management; (3) many leaders do believe that there is a need for planning; (4) many of the identifiable failures cannot be blamed solely on unforseen and uncontrollable factors; and (5) the demands of a volatile environment for NFPs supports, overall, a growing urgency for the planning concept.

The philosophy of this book is that in order for everyone in the not-for-profit organization–the board, the executive director, the membership–to be successful, a strategic plan is desperately needed. If you look at the mistakes of the past, it is obvious that many not-for-profits have floundered because they lack strategic direction. Over years of consulting with these types of organizations, the authors have observed this exact pattern in a large number of them. If you take the time and effort to study this book, follow up with your people, and apply the format prescribed here, this is what we believe you can expect:

1. A sense of enthusiasm in your organization
2. A five-year plan in writing to which everyone is committed
3. A sense of commitment by the entire organization to its overall direction
4. Clear job duties and responsibilities
5. Time for the leaders to do what they need to do
6. Clear and evident improvement in the health and vitality of every member of the organization's staff
7. Measurable improvement in the personal lives of all those in responsible positions with time for vacations, family, and personal pursuits
8. The ability to measure very specifically the growth and contribution made by administrators at the close of their careers
9. Guaranteed leadership of the not-for-profit because a plan is in

place in writing and is understood–even more important, a management team and philosophy will be in place to guide the organization into its next era of growth.

In this chapter we have presented our belief that strategic planning can improve managerial effectiveness in not-for-profit organizations. Such planning is particularly important since vast social questions and complex conditions in almost every community now demand the need for good management in these organizations.

The next chapter presents an overview of the entire strategic planning process. Then the following chapters cover each step of the planning process. The theory behind each step is presented, and actual examples are given to help understand that step. Make notes on your own situation as you read. Appendix A consolidates the worksheets found at the end of each chapter to prepare your strategic plan. Appendix A also displays an outline for presenting it. Read on with excitement!

REFERENCES

1. Byrne, John A. "Prepared, At Last," *Forbes* (October 10, 1983), pp. 32-33.

2. Jenster, P.V. and G. A. Overstreet, Jr. "Planning for a Non-profit Service: A Study of U.S. Credit Unions," *Long Range Planning,* Vol. 23, No. 2 (April, 1990), pp. 103-111.

3. "Preach the Gospel of Good Management," *Business Week* (March 26, 1990), p. 74.

4. Fottler, M.D., "Is Management Really Generic?" *Academy of Management Review,* (January, 1981), p. 2.

Chapter 2

Overview of Strategic Planning

"Cheshire Puss," she [Alice] began . . . "Would you please tell me which way I ought to go from here?"
"That depends on where you want to get to," said the cat.

Lewis Carroll
Alice in Wonderland

The problem is that the non-profits don't react in a rational way, the way a businessman would. They haven't the basic underlying concern that they can go out of business. They fool themselves. If you start off with that premise, spending money becomes a lot less difficult.

Alan Miller
Chairman, Universal Health Services

We have limited resources, which means we have to manage them even better to achieve the best results.

James A. Osborne
National Commander, The Salvation Army

This chapter presents an overview of the strategic planning process. Each of the areas which are discussed in this chapter are dealt with in more detail in later chapters. The intention here is to provide an introduction to the major components of the process.

WHAT IS STRATEGIC PLANNING?

The word strategic means, "pertaining to strategy." Strategy is derived from the Greek word *strategos* which means generalship, art of the general, or more broadly, leadership. The word strategic when used in the context of planning provides a perspective to planning which is long-run in nature and deals with achieving specified end results. Just as military strategy has as its objective the winning of the war, so too, strategic planning has as its goal the achievement of your organization's purpose–service to your clients.

Strategic decisions must be differentiated from tactical decisions. Strategic decisions outline the overall game plan or approach, while tactical decisions involve implementing various activities which are needed to carry out the larger strategy. For example, a service organization which decides to change locations because of shifting population trends and industrial development around the present location is making strategic decisions. Then many other decisions must be made about the exact location, size of building, parking facilities, and other major details. These all have long-term implications and are therefore strategic in nature.

Then other decisions such as wall colors, decor, and whether or not to have air conditioning must be made. These are tactical decisions needed to carry out or implement the strategic decision previously made. Thus, strategic decisions provide the overall framework within which the tactical decisions are made. It is critically important that leaders of not-for-profit organizations be able to differentiate between these types of decisions to identify whether the decision has short-term or long-term implications.

THE STRATEGIC PLANNING PROCESS

The strategic planning process is basically a matching process involving an NFP's internal resources and its external opportunities. The objective of this process is to peer through the "strategic window" and identify opportunities the individual organization is equipped to take advantage of or respond to. Thus the strategic management process can be defined as *a managerial process which involves matching the not-for-profit's capabilities with its opportunities.* These opportunities are identified over time and decisions revolve around investing or divesting resources to address these opportunities. The context in which these strategic decisions are made is: (1) the NFP's operating environment; (2) the NFP's purpose or mission; and (3) the NFP's organization-wide objectives. Strategic planning is the process which ties all these elements together to facilitate strategic choices which are consistent with all three areas and then implements and evaluates these choices. Appendix A presents an outline of a strategic plan.

The successful results of planning described earlier can be achieved through implementing an effective strategic planning process. The following breakdown of this process is a complete outline of a system capable of creating true change in your NFP's attitudes as well as in its productivity.

It is important to recognize at this point what we call "the two Ps." The first "P" means Product: get the plan in writing. The plan must be something you can hold in your hand, a written product of your efforts. If the plan is not in writing, it is called daydreaming. When it is in writing, you are telling yourself and others you are serious about it. The second "P" represents Process: every plan must have maximum input from everyone. Those who execute the plan must be involved in construction of the plan in order to gain their commitment. The best way to ensure a plan's failure is to overlook both the product and the process. They are equally important.

While there are many different ways in which an NFP can approach the strategic planning process, a systematic approach that carries the organization through a series of integral steps helps focus attention on answering a basic set of questions each organization must answer:

1. *What will we do?* This question focuses attention on the specific needs the NFP will try to meet.
2. *Who will we do it for?* This question addresses the need for an NFP to identify the various groups whose needs will be met.
3. *How will we do what we want to do?* Answering this question forces thinking about the many avenues through which an NFP's efforts may be channeled.

The strategic planning process used by an organization must force the NFP's leadership to deal with these questions on a continuous basis. Ongoing answers to these most fundamental questions allow the organization to continuously adapt over time and do the work it is best suited to do.

Strategic planning is defined as a process that involves completing the following steps.

1. Defining an organization's purpose and reason for being.
2. Analyzing environment opportunities and threats, assessing the NFP's own strengths and weaknesses, and making assumptions about future operating conditions.
3. Prescribing written, specific, and measurable objectives in the principal result areas that contribute to the organization's purpose.
4. Developing strategies on how to use available resources to meet objectives.
5. Developing operational plans to meet objectives including plans for all individuals in the organization.
6. Setting up control and evaluation procedures to determine if performance is keeping pace with attainment of objectives and if it is consistent with defined purpose.

The six steps of the strategic planning process are illustrated in Exhibit 2-1. They are important because they force the organization to consider certain questions. As each step requires the people at various organizational levels to discuss, study, and negotiate, the process as a whole fosters a planning mentality. When the six steps are complete, the end result is a strategic plan for the organization specifying why the organization exists, what it is trying to accomplish, and how resources will be utilized to accomplish objectives and fulfill its purpose. Let us briefly describe each of the six planning stages.

Defining Purpose

The first and probably the most important consideration when developing a strategic plan is to define the purpose, mission, or the "reason for being" of the organization or any specific part of it.

EXHIBIT 2-1. Strategic Planning Process

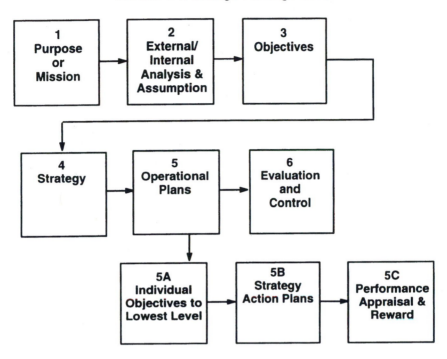

This is usually a difficult process even though it may appear simple. Multiple, often diverse views of the NFP's fundamental purpose may exist because of the differing perspectives of the numerous constituencies that hold a stake in the performance of the organization. Nevertheless, as Peter Drucker, noted management authority, emphasizes, "The best nonprofits devote a great deal of thought to defining their organization's mission."[1]

For example, a not-for-profit which defines itself as "a group of volunteers who help the needy" may be on the right track but will constantly face the need to explain and expand this definition. Does "help" mean only offer financial assistance or does it also include clothing, shelter, food, and health care? If these other services, like health care, are added to the definition, will health services involve only traditional physical care or will other needs be addressed, such as psychological counseling or substance abuse treatment? Granted these things may change as the organization evolves and grows; but thinking through these issues provides a sense of vision and also avoids going off on tangential activities which do not fit with what the organization wants to do or be.

The purpose statement should present the dream and vision of what the organization aspires to be. Members should try to visualize what they want the organization to become. If they can see where they are going and have an image of the real mission of the organization, their plans will fall into place more easily.

A vision of what can be accomplished creates the spark and energy for the whole planning and management process. It is important to spend ample time defining this purpose statement. The process should emphasize getting everyone involved in the dream of how things can be. Without a vision, people just work day-to-day and tend not to be as productive or willing to go all out.

In addition, a good statement of purpose not only clarifies what the NFP does, it sets boundaries. It defines what the organization will not do. It helps limit expectations, and that alone can make it the NFP administrator's best friend.

Analysis and Assumptions

It is vital for the not-for-profit to gauge the environment within which it operates. This should be standard practice for all NFPs. The only way we can manage change is to constantly monitor the environment within which we operate. This analysis stage is where we look at the environment external to our organization for potential threats and opportunities, and at our internal operation for strengths and weaknesses.

For example, some "downtown" hospitals have faced a dilemma of whether to remain in the downtown area or move to the suburbs. In these instances, the NFPs found that their historic location resulted in two significant problems: lack of space to grow and a change in the socioeconomic makeup of the neighborhood. The socioeconomic changes made the organization less effective in meeting the needs of those in the neighborhood who were less able to afford health care services. Potential patients with greater ability to afford care had moved and now sought care closer to their new homes.

Their solution was quite interesting. Downtown hospitals bought land and built satellite hospitals in growing parts of their community. Everybody won! The old neighborhood hospitals could serve the needs of those who lived there, while the new hospitals were built in an area where they could grow and help fund care at the inner city facilities. Some strategic thinking churches have made similar moves with success.

Many organizations have found it useful to use an analysis framework referred to earlier as a SWOT analysis. SWOT is an acronym for strengths, weaknesses, opportunities, and threats. Strengths and weaknesses refer to elements internal to the organization while opportunities and threats are external to the organization. A detailed SWOT analysis helps the NFP take a good look at the organization's favorable and unfavorable factors with a view toward building on strengths and eliminating or minimizing weaknesses. At the same time, the NFP's leadership must also assess external opportunities which could be pursued and threats which must be dealt with in order to survive.

The next stage is to state your major assumptions. These should be made about situations over which you have little or absolutely no control, such as the external environment. One good place to start is to extend some of the items studied in the external analysis. Should this stage appear relatively unimportant in developing a strategic plan, consider this: by not making explicit assumptions you are making one major implicit assumption–things are going to remain the same and nothing that happens is important enough to affect you!

Establishing Objectives

Often the words "key results," "goals," and "targets" are used synonymously with objectives when thinking about long- and short-term objectives. Think of an archer drawing an arrow and aiming directly at a target. The bulls-eye represents exactly where you want to be at a certain point in time. Administrators want their whole organization aimed at the same target just as an archer wants his arrow aimed at the target. At the other extreme, an archer that shoots his arrows off in any direction is liable to hit almost anything–including the wrong target. People get confused and disorganized if they do not know where they are going.

Objectives must be clear, concise, written statements outlining what is to be accomplished in key priority areas, over a certain time period, in measurable terms that are consistent with the overall purpose of the organization. Objectives are the results desired upon completion of the planning period. In the absence of objectives, no sense of direction can be attained in decision making. A basic truism is: "If you don't know where you are going, any road will get you there." In planning, objectives answer one of the basic questions posed in the planning process: Where do we want to go? These objectives become the focal point for strategy decisions.

Another basic purpose served by objectives is in the evaluation of performance. Objectives in the strategic plan become the yardsticks used to evaluate performance. As will be pointed out later, it is impossible to evaluate performance without some standard against which results can be compared. The objectives become the standards for evaluating performance because they are the statement of results desired by the planner.

Strategy Development

After developing a set of objectives for the time period covered by the strategic plan, the methods or strategy needed to accomplish those objectives must be formulated. This is accomplished in stages.

First, strategy alternatives must be developed and alternate courses of action evaluated by management before commitment is made to a specific option. From these, an overall strategy can be designed. Then operational strategies for each of our major service areas can be developed to detail activities to accomplish the grand strategy. In so doing, strategy becomes the link between objectives and results.

Operational Plans

After these steps have been taken and a strategy has been developed to meet your objectives and goals, it is time to develop an operational or action plan. The operational plan stage is the "action" or "doing" stage. Here you hire, fire, build, advertise, and so on. How many times has a group of people planned something, gotten enthusiastic and nothing happened? This is usually because they did not complete an operational or action plan to implement their strategy.

Operational plans need to be developed in all the areas that are used to support the overall strategy. These include operations, communications, finance, and staffing. Each of these more detailed plans is designed to spell out what needs to happen in a given area to implement the strategic plan.

Supporting the operational plans are the individual plans of all members of the organization. These are shown as steps 5A, 5B, and 5C in the model (see Exhibit 2-1). When planning is carried from the top to the lowest level in the organization, everyone becomes involved in negotiating and setting personal objectives which support the organization's objectives. Then individuals begin to develop their own action plans which are used to accomplish their objectives. Finally, the personal performance appraisal which must be done on an individual basis uses those individual objectives as the basis of appraisal and reward.

Evaluation and Control

Failure to establish procedures to appraise and control the strategic plan can lead to less than optimal performance. A plan is not complete until the controls are identified, and the procedures for recording and transmitting control information to the administrators of the plan are established. Many organizations fail to understand the importance of establishing procedures to appraise and control the planning process. Control should be a natural follow-through in developing a plan.

Planning and control should be integral processes. The strategic planning process results in a strategic plan. This plan is implemented (activities are performed in the manner described in the plan), and results are produced. These results may be reflected in services rendered, financial sponsorship, volunteer participation, and image enhancement.

Information on these and other key result areas can be used by administrators, to compare the results with original objectives to evaluate performance. This performance evaluation identifies the areas where decisions must be made to adjust activities, people, or finances. The actual decision making controls the plan by altering it to accomplish stated objectives, and a new cycle begins.

Individual performance appraisal is a vital part of this step. Rewards or reprimands must be related to the personal achievement or lack of achievement of agreed upon objectives. This creates a work environment where people know what to do and rewards are tied to performance.

STRATEGIC PLANNING AS AN ONGOING PROCESS

Strategic planning is not simply a singular event to be repeated only every three to five years. The word "process" can be defined as a series of actions or operations conducing to an end. Here, we wish to emphasize the ongoing action aspect of the planning process. The actions are the activities in which the NFP engages to accomplish objectives and fulfill its mission, and they must continually evolve.

There are several important reasons for viewing strategic planning as a process. First is the idea that a process can be studied and improved. A not-for-profit just getting involved in strategic planning will need to review the whole process on an annual basis, not only to account for changing environmental forces, but to improve or refine the plan. Purpose statements, objectives, strategies, and appraisal techniques can be fine tuned over time as the planners gain more experience and as new and better information becomes available.

A second reason for viewing strategic planning as a process is that a change in any component of the process will affect most or all of the other components. For example, a change in purpose or objective will lead to new analysis, strategies, and evaluations. Thus, major changes which affect the organization must lead to a reevaluation of all the elements of the plan.

Finally, and perhaps most important, is that involvement in the strategic planning process can become the vehicle through which the whole organization mobilizes its energies to accomplish its purpose. If all members of the organization can participate in the process in some way, an atmosphere can be created within the organization that implies that doing the right things and doing things right is everybody's job. Participation instills ownership. It's not "my plan" or "their plan," but "our plan" that becomes important; everyone will *want* to make a contribution to make it happen.

STRATEGY IMPLEMENTATION

The focus of this book is on the strategic planning process which results in the development of a strategic plan. This plan becomes the blueprint for carrying out the many activities in which an NFP is involved. There are many other issues that determine the effectiveness of an organization that are beyond the scope of this book. These issues essentially revolve around implementing the strategic plan through (1) staffing and training personnel and volunteers, (2) developing organizational relationships among staff/volunteers, (3) achieving commitment, (4) developing a positive organizational culture, (5) discovering the most effective leadership styles, and (6) emloying personnel evaluation and reward systems.

Our lack of discussion of these topics is due to space limitation and a desire to keep the length of the book "manageable" for readers. Both effective planning and implementation are needed to create an effective organization. The strategic plan concentrates on "doing the right things" while implementation concentrates on "doing things right." Examples of two entire strategic plans for NFPs are presented in Appendix B.

SUMMARY

This chapter has presented an overview of the strategic planning process in which a series of thought-provoking questions must be answered. The process is a set of integral steps which carries the planners through a sequence that involves providing answers to these questions and then continually rethinking and reevaluating these answers as the organization and its environment change.

A helpful tool to use at this stage is Section I of the Strategic Planning Worksheets located at the end of this chapter and in Appendix A. This form, when thoughtfully filled out, will provide an assessment of your current position in terms of planning and management of your organization. It will help point out where to direct your efforts as you work to improve the efficiency and effectiveness of the organization entrusted to your leadership.

REFERENCE

1. Drucker, P.F. "What Business Can Learn From Non-Profits," *Harvard Business Review,* (July-August, 1989), p. 89.

PLANNING PROCESS WORKSHEET

This worksheet is provided to aid your not-for-profit organization in starting the strategic planning process. Use the answers to these questions to provide a foundation for completing the remaining worksheets.

1. Who should be involved in the planning process?

   _____

   _____

   _____

2. Where will planning sessions be held?

   _____

   _____

   _____

3. When will planning sessions be held?

   _____

   _____

   _____

4. What types of background material do participants need prior to starting the first session?

   _____

   _____

   _____

5. Who will lead the process? Who will ultimately be responsible for arranging sessions, and getting material typed, reproduced, and distributed?

   _____

   _____

   _____

6. When and how will the staff, board, membership, or others be involved in the process?

_____

_____

_____

7. How will the results be communicated to everyone in the organization?

_____

_____

_____

8. Who will train/supervise staff members in working with their own staff and volunteers in setting objectives, developing action plans, and conducting performance appraisals?

_____

_____

_____

9. How frequently will the process be reviewed and by whom?

_____

_____

_____

10. Who will be responsible for dealing with external groups (sponsors, media, consultants) in preparing the plan?

_____

_____

_____

Chapter 3

Defining Organizational Purpose

However brilliant an action may be, it should not be accounted great when it is not the result of a great purpose.

Francois De La Rochefoucauld

If you're the Girl Scouts, IBM, or AT&T, you have to manage for a mission.

Frances Hesselbein
Former Executive Director, Girl Scouts of America

The best nonprofits devote a great deal of thought to defining their organization's mission.

Peter Drucker
Management Expert

This chapter outlines the first step in the strategic planning process: defining your purpose or mission. Without a clear and carefully considered statement of purpose all other stages of the process will be misguided. Accordingly, we will discuss the value of defining the not-for-profit's purpose, describe how to write effective mission statements, and present examples of mission statements.

THE IMPORTANCE OF DEFINING PURPOSE

The first and probably most important consideration when developing a strategic plan is to define the purpose, mission, or the "reason for being" for the organization or any specific part of it. This is usually a difficult process. Peter Drucker, management consultant and writer, has led the way in stressing the importance of defining purpose. Drucker notes the importance of identifying an organization's purpose by emphasizing that it is the process of organizing to satisfy a need in the marketplace. The mission concept should be client-oriented in that it is defined by the want the customer satisfies when he buys a product or a service. Thus, satisfying the customer is the mission and purpose of every business.[1]

Organizations need a clear definition of purpose and mission because that is the only way to obtain clear and realistic business objectives. It is the foundation for priorities, strategies, plans and work assignments. The mission is the starting point for the design of managerial structure and jobs.[2]

Clearly, if purpose is defined casually or introspectively, the basis for how an organization goes about achieving its objectives rests on shaky foundations. If we do not know what we are about, then anything we do, regardless of its true effectiveness, can be made to sound like it was the best course of action. This can be self-deluding and self-defeating, taking us away from the long-run basis for our existence: meeting client needs. As Calvin Coolidge put it: "No enterprise can exist for itself alone. It ministers to some great need, it performs some great service not for itself but for others; or failing therein it ceases to be profitable and ceases to exist."

It is not always easy to formulate a statement of purpose. The purpose statement should have the dream and vision of what the organization wants to be. Members should try to visualize what they want the organization to be. If they can see where they are going and have an image of the real mission of the organization, the implementation of their plans will fall more easily into place.

It is important to understand this concept of purpose and vision in order to have a successful NFP operation. The vision is what unites your staff and volunteers and spurs them to higher performance. Without a long-term perspective an NFP will continually swerve off course instead of moving with steadiness and certainty toward its goals.

It is in this purpose statement that the vision and the dream for the NFP must be reflected. This purpose statement sets the stage for all planning. A clear mission statement provides a starting point for determining goals and objectives as specific measures of mission effectiveness.

Objectives, which are covered later in the text, must by their very nature contribute to achieving what is in the purpose statement. Without objectives a mission statement becomes an empty platitude. Too often this link is missed. For example, in a study of private Christian college and university administrations, it was discovered that all those surveyed had a purpose and mission statement, but only 50 percent had specific measurable objectives of what was to be accomplished.

In summary, six reasons may be suggested for a not-for-profit to have a mission statement:

1. It provides a reason for being, an explanation to ourselves and others as to why we exist as an organization.
2. It sets boundaries around our operations and thus defines what we will do and what we will not do.
3. It describes the need we are attempting to meet in the world and how we are going to respond to that need.
4. It acts as the foundation on which the primary objectives of the organization can be based.
5. It helps to form the basis for the ethos (or culture) of the organization.
6. It helps us to communicate to those outside the organization what we are all about.

BASIC ELEMENTS COVERED IN A MISSION STATEMENT

In developing a mission statement, several basic elements should be reflected:

1. *History.* Every organization has a history which includes past problems, accomplishments, objectives and policies. The mission statement should reflect the historical significance of such characteristics.
2. *Distinctive competencies.* This element reflects what the organization is uniquely equipped to do because of its location,

personnel, resources, or historical position. While most organizations can do many things, they can do some things so well that they have an advantage over other organizations in certain areas.

3. *Needs, segments, and technology.* The mission statement must reflect what we will do (needs met or values received by clients), who we will do it for (client groups or segments to be served since we cannot be all things to all people), and what technology will be used (how needs will be met).

4. *Environment.* Each organization operates in an environment that dictates the opportunities and threats which must be dealt with when a mission statement is developed. Laws structuring insurance policies, and fear of diseases transmitted are examples of environmental factors which influence an organization's ability to achieve its purpose.

It is not unusual for an organization to work on a mission statement for months or even years before deciding that it really reflects what the organization wants to become. Once developed, the mission statement is not a once and forever document. As the NFP adapts itself to the demands of a changing environment, so should the mission statement reflect this adaptation. It must be reviewed periodically and updated appropriately to continually reflect the NFP's fundamental purposes. This is a difficult and thought-provoking process when approached correctly, but it must be done. As stated earlier, what an organization does (objectives and strategies) should flow from what the organization is (mission or purpose).

WRITING A STATEMENT OF PURPOSE

The following list provides several helpful tips on writing and evaluating a purpose statement:

1. Determine your fundamental reason for being. For an NFP under development, this means expressly determining what need satisfaction you will offer your client. If your NFP is currently operating and not a new start-up, this means moving your thinking beyond simply what you now do. You must specifically identify what the need satisfaction *should* be for

your NFP. Identifying your basic purpose for existence also means wrestling with what need satisfaction your NFP may be offering in the future.

One outcome of these considerations should be a section of the statement that is specific enough to offer guidance to the NFP's membership in the near term. But there should also be a general aspect that looks to the future and provides "wiggle room" for your NFP to adapt and grow with future needs. Done effectively, these aspects of the mission statement serve as a touchstone, reminding the NFP membership why they do what they do.

2. Identify your principal methods for delivering need satisfaction. This issue focuses on the basic activities and functions your NFP will employ to meet the needs of your clientele. Verbs are the key here. "Make" or "manufacture," and "market," "provide," "offer," or "serve" are all action words representative of basic delivery activities. Here, the NFP must deal with the issue of to what extent it will develop products or services in-house as opposed to acquiring them from outside sources and then coordinating their delivery in a way that provides value to the client.

3. Determine the scope of your mission. This involves determining who you intend to serve. Proper deliberation here focuses attention outside the nuts and bolts of internal activities. It forces consideration of the intended recipients of your NFP's functions. At a practical level, scope identifies the breadth of delivery–local neighborhood, community-wide, regional, national, or international. If your operation is part of a larger organization, the parent organization becomes part of your clientele served since your mission should support the parent organization's purpose on the one hand, and be accountable to it on the other. In effect, you are writing a mission for your unit that delivers on the larger organization's purpose for a constituency that is smaller than that of the parent organization. For instance, the American Red Cross has a mission that seeks to serve an entire nation. But a local Red Cross chapter should define its mission in terms of applying the national purpose to a specific constituency such as the local community.

4. Determine that portion of the above mission statement for which your unit is accountable. While the American Red Cross' national mission might include many services such as blood supplies, tissue services, and emergency services, a local chapter's capabilities may be more limited, excluding, for instance, tissue services. Your mission statement should reflect these differences where they exist.

5. Prepare a rough draft of the mission statement that covers the purpose of the group and the major activities it performs. With a working team, such as the administrative staff and board of directors, a rough draft mission statement can be developed at an all-day meeting, using an outside facilitator who is familiar with communications techniques, group processes, and the concept of mission statements. The meeting can begin with each individual writing his own version of the mission statement on newsprint. When these drafts are all assembled, the group can review each one for clarity and understanding. Finally, condense those portions that are similar so that only areas of wide disagreement are left. At this point, negotiations can be carried out between members of the group until there is general agreement on all points ("I am able to live with this"). The final result is the rough draft of the mission statement.

SAMPLE MISSION STATEMENTS

It might be helpful at this point to examine some mission statements prepared by various local and regional chapters of not-for-profit organizations. Note that these statements reflect the uniqueness of the organizations in terms of their reason for being and also serve as guidelines for what the organization should be doing. These statements were developed through a process involving many people. Initial statements were revised many times to add specificity and clarity to the terms used to define purpose.

A Salvation Army Unit

The Salvation Army, founded in 1865, is an international religious and charitable movement organized and operated on a quasi-military pattern and is a branch of the Christian church. Its membership includes officers (clergy), soldiers-adherents (laity), members of varied activity groups and volunteers who serve as advisors, associates and committed participants in its service functions.

The motivation of the organization is love of God and a practical concern for the needs of humanity. This is expressed by a spiritual ministry, the purposes of which are to preach the Gospel, disseminate Christian truths, supply basic human necessities, provide personal counseling and undertake the spiritual and moral regeneration and physical rehabilitation of all persons in need who come within its sphere of influence regardless of race, color, creed, sex, or age.

An Area Goodwill Industry Unit

The purpose of the corporation is to improve the quality of life of individuals with disabilities and other barriers to employment and independence by expanding their vocational opportunities, occupational capacities and integrated community living opportunities through a network of services in response to local needs; and, to engage in any other lawful act or activity for which corporations may be organized under the general corporation laws of the state.

A Drug Abuse Program

The mission of the Drug Abuse Program is to provide free support and counseling to young people, families and communities of the city, county and surrounding area who are experiencing hardships and problems related to drug and alcohol abuse.

We, the Board of Trustees, staff, and volunteers of the program, pledge to actively seek the fulfillment of this mission and in order to do so will seek to:

- Provide viable, and effective solutions to young people and families suffering from the effect of drug and alcohol abuse.
- Offer informational and educational services that are of the highest quality.
- Provide and/or promote sound prevention models that address area youth, families and communities.

We also understand that undertaking this task, we assume the additional responsibility of protecting/preserving the effectiveness and good name now historically associated with the Drug Abuse Program. In doing so, the program's traditions and means of operating should always be considered, so that objectives in meeting the missions statement do not conflict with already proven success. Be it not mistaken, this endeavor is of selfless motivation and is hereby, dedicated to the health of our young people and to their families.

A Specialty School

Children's Place offers a second chance for success to Learning Disabled and Attention Deficit Disordered (with or without hyperactivity) children who have not succeeded in other public or private school special education programs. The purpose of our school is to help each child compensate for his or her specific learning disabilities, increase the child's self-esteem, self-confidence, and social skills, and return the child to a traditional school classroom as quickly as possible, prepared to achieve his or her full potential. We strive to constantly provide the highest quality individualized educational services in the state for these special children, who are in pre-school (four years of age) through eighth grade.

The mission of the School is to create a stronger community by helping children with special educational needs not only overcome their disabilities, but develop the critical thinking and life skills necessary to their becoming responsible, productive adults.

An American Heart Association Chapter

The mission of the American Heart Association is to reduce death and disability due to cardiovascular disease and stroke.

An Arts and Humanities Council

The Arts and Humanities Council was founded over a quarter of a century ago to nurture the creative forces within the community and to promote the knowledge and appreciation of both the arts and the humanities for the citizens of the metropolitan region. Through education and public programs, the Council strives to make experiences in the arts and humanities a conscious part of everyone's life.

In pursuit of its mission, the Council does not impose a single aesthetic standard or attempt to direct artistic content.

A Regional Arthritis Foundation Chapter

The mission of this regional Arthritis Foundation chapter is: to provide information and education about arthritis, its related diseases, as well as chapter programs and services; to provide an appropriate range of quality services to those individuals and families affected by these diseases; and to work with professionals involved in the diagnosis and treatment of arthritis-related diseases through the provision of education, information, and funding of research.

In order to accomplish this mission and to support the efforts of the National Arthritis Foundation, the chapter actively solicits contributions of time, resources, and financial support.

A Domestic Violence Intervention Service

DVIS By-Laws state: "The general purpose . . . is to stop domestic violence by providing a wide array of primary and secondary prevention counseling, advocacy and education services. The agency assists battered women in taking control of their own lives and aids them in this process by providing shelter, advocacy and education services. DVIS believes that family violence is a public health problem which requires a comprehensive family-centered approach."

A Safety Council

The Safety Council is intended to be a focal point where industries, government and communities within the state can obtain safety and accident prevention information and services. The organization is exclusively an educational and training organization with the sole purpose of reducing the human suffering and economic losses resulting from unsafe conditions and unsafe actions.

A Drug Awareness Program

The mission of the Drug Awareness Program is to offer a quality prevention education program that deals directly with the root causes of drug and alcohol use/abuse and negative juvenile behavior. Our program educates the young and their parents about peer pressure and dealing with problems. The goal is to foster positive self-esteem and positive decision making, thereby making prevention a reality.

Area Council on Alcoholism and Drug Abuse

The Area Council on Alcoholism and Drug Abuse is an education, information agency providing health and wellness programs that helps build capable, responsible, independent people thereby reducing the risk and the incidence of the dependencies of alcoholism or other drug abuse. The goal of ACADA is to help each client develop healthy perceptions and the skills which produce capabilities of self-confidence, judgment, responsibility, self-esteem, and therein increase his/her capacity to love and care for themselves.

Recreation Center for the Physically Limited

The goal of this corporation is to enable persons over the age of five with physical disabilities in the metropolitan area to enhance their lives. To this end, we offer opportunities for growth and self-fulfillment in a recreational setting.

In recognition of the fact that this commitment to the quest for a fuller life by persons with physical disabilities cannot be met solely within the confines of our program or facility, we additionally recognize our responsibility for becoming aware of and addressing the issues important to persons with physical disabilities within the community as a whole. To accomplish this aim, while concentrating on our primary program of growth through recreation, we will seek to participate in cooperative efforts with other groups and agencies actually and potentially representing and/or serving citizens with physical disabilities.

In summary, a purpose statement needs to be built around several points:

1. *Internal operations and functions*–typically this includes a description of the fundamental activities the not-for-profit engages in, specifically, the basic services provided such as education, training, counseling, clothing, housing, and so on. This aspect of the statement thus answers the "what do we do?" question.
2. *External clientele*–this part of the statement focuses on identifying the customers to be served by the NFP. This may include descriptions of demographic characteristics (such as, the homeless) as well as geographic boundaries (such as the Dallas, Texas metropolitan area). This portion of the statement emphasizes answers to the "who do we serve?" question.
3. *Needs served*–the emphasis here is on the needs of constituencies that will be met. These are the ultimate ends we hope to achieve such as better health, more productive citizenry, a greater appreciation of the arts, and so on. Philosophically, this section identifies who we are and hope to be, giving our mem-

bership an identity to hold on to in uncertain times and the leeway to stretch toward new services and greater goal attainment of existing ones.

EVALUATING A PURPOSE STATEMENT

The list below can be used as a guide to evaluate a statement of purpose. The idea is to come up with a statement that really represents what the organization wants to be or should be to survive.

1. Broadness and continuity of application: The statement should be broad enough to cover all significant areas of activity expected of the organization without a specific termination period indicated.
2. Functional commitment: The nature of the works, tasks, or activities to be performed must be defined in terms that will determine clearly the validity of the group or organization.
3. Resource commitment: The statement should include a commitment to cost-effective utilization of available resources.
4. Unique or distinctive nature of work: Every unit in an organization should make some unique or distinctive contribution. If there are two or more units in an organization with identical mission statements, the risk of duplicated effort is obvious.
5. Description of services to be offered.
6. Description of group or groups to be served.
7. Geographical area to be covered.

Sometimes it is useful to use a series of questions to evaluate a purpose statement after it is written. A "no" answer to one of the questions means the statement needs to be reworded to more clearly reflect the organization's basic reason for being. The following lists of questions may be useful to you.

1. Does it contain all important commitments?
2. Does it clearly state the function?
3. Is there a clear determination of relationships to any parent organization?
4. Is it distinct from the mission statements of other groups in the organization?

5. Is it short, to the point, and understandable?
6. Is it continuing in nature?
7. Does it state to whom the group is accountable?

While the word "service" is often included in the mission statement of many organizations, fundamentally the purpose statement needs to answer specifically the question of why your organization is needed in the first place. Plenty of other organizations exist. Discuss and know clearly what needs you are meeting and for whom. In answering the "for whom" question, a purpose statement can reflect whether the NFP wants to be local, regional, national or international.

For example, The Arts and Humanities Council, noted earlier, targets its local community promoting appreciation of the arts. Similarly, the Drug Abuse Program described above determined that it exists to meet substance abuse support and counseling needs for the surrounding area. The mission statement of the Arthritis Foundation chapter seeks to support national arthritis goals on a regional basis. The Salvation Army strives to transform needy individuals spiritually, physically, and civicly across the nation and the world.

SUMMARY

Hopefully, you have caught the significance of verbalizing and putting in writing the vision the leadership of your NFP has for its operation. By committing it to writing, you have, in effect, expressly stated the unique reason for your organization's existence. This provides the sense of identity, direction, and focus for what you do. What you do must be a function of who you are. The statement of purpose translates your long-run dreams and aspirations into tangible form and builds a stronger foundation for their fulfillment.

REFERENCES

1. Drucker, Peter. *Management: Tasks, Responsibilities, and Practice* (New York: Harper & Row), 1974, p. 79.
2. Ibid., p. 75.

MISSION STATEMENT WORKSHEET

This worksheet will aid you in writing a mission statement for your not-for-profit organization.

1. Write a statement for the following areas:

    Internal operations statement: _____

    _____

    _____

    _____

    External clientele statement: _____

    _____

    _____

    _____

    Needs served statement: _____

    _____

    _____

    _____

2. Now evaluate the statement.

    Does it define boundaries within which your not-for-profit will operate?

    _____

    _____

    _____

    Does it define the need(s) that your NFP is attempting to meet?

    _____

    _____

    _____

    Do you intend to have local, regional, national, or international scope?

    _____

    _____

    _____

Does it define the market (clientele) that your NFP is reaching?

_____

_____

_____

Has there been input from appropriate organizational members?

_____

_____

_____

Does it include the word "service," or a word with similar meaning?

_____

_____

_____

3. Next, submit it to others familiar with your organization to evaluate your statement of purpose and offer suggestions on improving the statement. In other words, does the statement say to others what you want it to say?

_____

_____

_____

Chapter 4

Situation Analysis and Assumptions

You can never plan the future by the past.

Edmund Burke
English Statesman

A well-defined mission serves as a constant reminder of the need to look outside the organization not only for "customers" but also for measures of success.

Peter Drucker
Management Expert

We can no longer assume we know what our various constituencies need and want.

Sunshine Janda Overkamp
Senior Vice President, United Way of America

If you think what exists today is permanent and forever true, you inevitably get your head handed to you.

John Reed
Chairman, Citicorp

This chapter discusses the need to analyze the situation confronting the not-for-profit and to identify any assumptions on which the strategic plan will be based. We will first discuss the need to assess the environment within which the NFP operates to understand the nature of external influences. Next, the role of internal analysis of the situation within the NFP organization will be addressed. It is critical that all attributes (whether strengths or weaknesses) of the organization be understood as well as features of its external environment (consisting of opportunities and threats) in order to establish appropriate assumptions on which to develop plans. Consequently, this step in strategic planning is critical to the success of the process.

EXTERNAL ANALYSIS

It is vital for the not-for-profit to gauge the external environment within which it operates. This should be standard practice for all organizations. It is important to realize that anything that can happen ultimately probably will happen. Man truly can have no certain idea what things will be like in the future, in spite of our attempts to predict them.

The only way we can manage change is to constantly monitor the environment within which we operate. Examples for business might be the trends we see in gross national product, governmental control, regulation, the labor movement, interest rates, consumer preference, industry surveys, marketing research, Dow Jones stock averages, commodity prices, and so forth. Many of these same trends affect the not-for-profit organization.

This stage in the analysis is where we look at past and current developments external to our NFP's operations. From this we identify trends and, in effect, take the pulse of the environment in which the NFP operates. External analysis should not be confused with an assumption base which will be discussed later.

An NFP must be aware of characteristics of environmental conditions affecting it and be vigilant to changes that may occur in the business environment. There are numerous possible shifts that can occur to affect the firm: customers, economy, legalities, culture, and so forth. Many organizations have found that they failed to understand the implications of the environment on their actions and may not have heeded them, even when they were obvious.

Even without a formal organizational system to monitor the environment and changes in it, executives must exercise vigilance to detect and use information from the environment in formulating strategy.

Significance of Environmental Considerations

Organizational Failure May Result. Most management experts agree that any NFP, even one that is extremely successful, will be doomed to ultimate failure if it operates the way it has in the past. Why? Because the environment in which the organization operates is continually shifting and those factors leading to success in one environmental milieu may cause failure in another set of environmental circumstances.

Changes Will Occur. All of the environmental factors influencing the organization and its administration will change. This is a given. None of these factors stands still. Thus, the NFP administrator must expect change and should be receptive to it.

For instance, even the U.S. Postal Service, a fairly stable public sector bureaucracy, now faces a more turbulent environment. The advent of electronic mail, facsimile machines, computer networks, and such aggressive private sector competitors as UPS and Federal Express represent a much more complicated environment for mail delivery. Failure to be responsive to such changes means a less effective, even less relevant role for the U.S. mail. Other NFPs face similar brave new worlds with the consequences of inaction equally as dire.

Environmental Change Will Accelerate. The environment used to be considered an arena in which change was *evolutionary.* Today, however, changes are coming increasingly swiftly. We are now in a situation where changes could be considered *revolutionary.* One has only to look at the technological environment to appreciate this fact of rapid pace of change.

Recent significant management books are indicative of this rapid change as evidenced by their titles. Peter Drucker called this the *Age of Discontinuity,* and Alvin Toffler refers to the psychological condition a chaotically changing environment will bring about as *Future Shock.* Only now it is present shock.

Changes Will Be Significant. Environmental changes are certain to be significant. In every facet of the environment significant changes are afoot. Budget woes, health care costs/problems/aging of Americans, employment cutbacks/layoffs, global competition, worldwide recession, all signify significant changes that are occurring in the U.S. and the rest of the world.

Environmental Factors for Analysis

The environmental circumstances under which the organization is and will be operating in the future must be explicitly and carefully considered in any effective strategic planning. Given the nature of the environment, the administrator makes judgments about *opportunities* and *threats* facing the company. The opportunities must be capitalized upon and the threats avoided, minimized, or overcome in order to reach the organization's goals.

The external environmental analysis should evaluate at least seven factors:

1. Economic trends in your locality, in your geographic region, and in the nation. Examples of these trends are changes in personal income, employment, inflation, land values, and industry location.
2. Demographic trends including shifts in age groups, education levels, numbers of widows and retired people, and shifts of population to different geographic areas.
3. Community issues of urban versus suburban development, growth or decline of commercial activities, and transportation services.
4. Changes in the services offered to people in the community. Who is offering them? Are services primarily shifting into governmental hands or private sponsorship? How effective are these services in meeting the needs of the community?
5. Trends in competition from other NFPs for funding and for services which may overlap. What other things are going on that present you with competition at this time?
6. Volunteer recruitment trends in the community and region and reasons for changes in these trends. What NFP activities are proving to be the most popular at this time?
7. Changes in client needs and social values. Are your services what your clients truly need or will want? Apart from basic needs, how well do your services meet clients' expectations?

What do people in your community look on as being important? Are the services you offer valued?

As an example, a portion of an environmental analysis for an NFP hospital might include the following trends:

- The graying of America means more people under Medicare coverage as the baby boomers begin to reach old age. Demand for gerontology-related services will increase in parallel with this trend. Older people tend to be sicker and sick more often, driving the intensity of hospital services upward.
- Federal government reimbursement for Medicare patients is trending down. This complicates revenue planning and negatively impacts financial viability.
- Discussion of federal national health insurance programs are rampant in Washington, D.C. Congressional enactment could cause radical changes in reimbursement, if not delivery, of health care services.
- The costs of medical care continue to outpace inflation and have for two decades. Ford, Inc., now says it spends more for health care than for steel in its autos. As a result, large employers are now banding together and asking hospitals for discounts. Competing effectively for these contracts requires new information systems capable of tracking costs by company, by physician, as well as by diagnosis.
- Companies are using more part-time workers and cutting benefits costs by not offering health insurance. More patients without insurance drive up the cost of indigent care which still must be funded.
- Technological advances in diagnosis and treatment, such as magnetic resonance and positron emission tomography systems, are continuous and expensive to acquire and operate. Yet the latest in technology is necessary to recruit and maintain medical staff, the basic source of patients.
- Patients are increasingly expressing alarm at the costs of health care, indicating that even with health insurance, their families face potential personal financial ruin. Patients tend to delay seeking care due to high costs, which can mean they are indeed sicker when hospitalized and require more care.

- Philanthropy is drying up for hospitals. Changing tax laws regarding charitable contributions and changing patient attitudes toward hospitals' charges mean that more revenue must come directly from operations.
- NFP hospitals face increasing competition from for-profit hospital chains for the paying patient. Some for-profits tend to offer only the higher margin services, avoiding the financial drain experienced by NFPs from expensive, low volume services like neonatal intensive care. They can also buy in volume to control costs, while stand alone NFP hospitals cannot generate equivalent discounts with their lower usage.

Assessing Opportunities and Threats

Opportunities and threats related to the external environment are analyzed to determine if any action (strategy) is needed to deal with them. For example, a large number of homeless people in a downtown area could create an opportunity for a shelter to expand its operations, aiming directly at this group. Alternatively, the shelter organization may decide that, even though the opportunity exists, they do not have the resources to extend the service. In either case, opportunities cannot be pursued if they are not recognized and analyzed.

The same is true for threats. An NFP already in trouble from inadequate funding and in heavy debt would face even greater risks if it lost a key leader to illness or death without any preparation for a replacement. The "halo" effect of bad publicity regarding the management and expenses of other NFPs may also be a threat to the existence or at least the effectiveness of the not-for-profit organization. Recognizing such threats and analyzing the possible ramifications of events helps avoid many crises by developing contingency plans for dealing with such situations. Some have referred to this as "what if" and "what then" analysis. In other words, asking the questions of: "What if this happens?" and then "What do we do if this happens?" helps an NFP deal with major events which might be detrimental to the organization.

The more you know about the people being served, the better you can meet their needs. Thus the NFP's client base should be a prime element for study. Here, it is useful to build a data base. Many successful businesses, such as Wal-Mart, are continually doing research to learn more about their customers. An NFP should do the same thing. Information can be gathered on such factors as family size, marital status, age levels, where people work, people's needs, how long members have been using the NFP's services, housing and transportation used, and where they live. All of these are good questions to ask and know aggregate information about.

Scanning the environment of your NFP operation for significant trends, especially in changing times, is an ongoing effort. This stage in the planning process cannot be just gathering data, getting it on paper, and forgetting about it. The environment must be constantly monitored to help ensure your NFP's survival and growth.

INTERNAL ANALYSIS

After you have identified your NFP's purpose and considered the environment in which you operate, it is important to objectively assess the strengths and weaknesses of your NFP's internal operations. NFP administrators need to learn from athletic coaches in this area. They are constantly assessing the strengths and weaknesses of their team and the opponent. They try to maximize their strengths on game day, and during practice improve on their weaknesses.

Organizations have certain strengths which make them uniquely suited to carry out their tasks. Conversely, they have certain weaknesses which inhibit their abilities to fulfill their purposes. NFPs that seek greater effectiveness need to carefully evaluate the strengths and weaknesses of their organizations.

Identifying strengths and weaknesses within the organization involves a thorough internal analysis, or strategic audit, of the organization. A complete study of the NFP's emphasis on its services and how well they are delivered is the goal. In looking for strengths and weaknesses in the functioning of your organization, a strength is some significant aspect of your operations that is done exceedingly well. What we mean by significant operational aspect is some fundamental activity that is highly likely to affect the performance of your NFP in a major way. Conversely, a weakness is some inadequacy in a major activity or resource that reduces the firm's ability to achieve its goals.

Several different benchmarks can be used to identify whether an activity should be considered a strength or a weakness. One internal standard is how well this activity meets its operational goals when compared to other major functions. This comparison can be made over time to establish trends in effectiveness. Another standard is how well our NFP handles this activity when compared with this function in other NFPs which might be considered our immediate competitors. This is called a strategic group comparison. Another important benchmark for NFPs in particular is how well the activity contributes to the NFP's ability to satisfy the expectations of our funding sponsor. But perhaps the most fundamental standard is how well this activity meets the immediate and long-term needs and interests of our clients.

Assessing Strengths and Weaknesses: The Search for a Distinctive Competence

The definitive goal of an internal strengths and weaknesses analysis is to identify a distinctive competence. A distinctive competence is some function that we do extraordinarily well. It represents a level of mastery which makes our NFP extremely effective in meeting client needs particularly when we consider the typical effectiveness of our strategic group in this area of operation. In other words, a distinctive competence is a super strength that give us an edge in delivering client satisfaction.

A systematic way to identify strengths and weaknesses is to divide your NFP's operations into major sectors for analysis. Depending on the specific nature of your organization, some basic categories for internal analysis include overall management effectiveness and firm resources, financial operations, marketing operations, and operations or service functions. A good place to begin is with the management of the NFP and its planning systems.

Management and Planning Systems. A specific target of a strengths and weaknesses analysis should be a study of the management system. Management's willingness to take risks, and its values, skills, age, and experience are all important aspects of an organization's ability to respond to opportunities. Identifying the effectiveness of an NFP's human resources management is also an objective of this portion of the analysis. This can include issues of how well the firm is organized, as well as staff turnover and the recruitment and morale of volunteers.

For instance, the demographics of our volunteers are important in understanding volunteer effectiveness. Appropriate questions include the following. How many people do we have in each age group? What are the basic categories of jobs and income levels? What percentage of volunteers consists of retired people or widows?

Still another target for analysis concerns our organization's culture or personality. The following questions deal with the organizational culture profile of our NFP. Are we conservative or liberal in our service philosophy? Are we client driven or do we focus more on financial sponsors' expectations? Does our NFP collaborate with other community agencies and institutions? As an NFP organization, what are our primary interests and social values? What is the power structure of our NFP? Who makes the decisions and by what process?

Also important to analyze is the effectiveness of our present programs. What are they? Is the leadership for each program effective? How much interest and support does each program have? A management questionnaire can be developed which provides information on the effectiveness of the management system and brings major problems to the surface.

Another target of this analysis is the planning system. Is planning undertaken systematically and performed on a regular basis? Are contingency plans considered? Are the plans realistic? Are they in fact used? All are important issues. Again, a questionnaire can be used to identify and review the planning environment and process, organizational structure, management philosophy and style as it relates to planning, and other planning factors relating to the organization's performance.

The result is a thorough understanding of the planning system. The data collected in the audit can then be analyzed to determine strengths and weaknesses in the planning system. The most important are then included in a strengths and weaknesses summary as a portion of the overall strategic audit. In a similar fashion, the following sectors can be analyzed using surveys and the major findings incorporated into the audit.

Financial Resources. The total amount of financial resources an organization has available and the process through which these funds are allocated influence the organization's ability to function effectively. For some organizations there are insurmountable financial barriers. Not only are capital needs extensive, but other expenditures are at a high level. Adequate financial resources must be available to insure the provision of adequate production and marketing capabilities or the organization must have easy access to funding sources before some opportunities can be undertaken.

Adequate initial financial resources are needed to operate in many cases for the first few years while enough paying clients or funding sponsors are developed to sustain an operation. Low revenue levels and high operating costs during the first few years must be anticipated. It goes without saying that unless the financial resources to permit continued operation are available, failure can be anticipated. Thus, an organization's current financial position plus its ability to successfully obtain financing directly influence its ability to pursue opportunities.

Specifically, financial resources of the NFP–including operating funds, special funds, donations, and expenditures–should be analyzed. Appropriate questions include the following. What has been our performance over the last five years in adhering to budget limits? What is our ability to raise funds when needed? Other specific targets for analysis include breakeven points, cash flow, and debt-to-asset ratios.

Marketing Resources. An organization's ability to take advantage of opportunities requires personnel with the marketing skills necessary to develop and execute effective marketing strategies. A good service does not guarantee success. The old adage "Build a better mousetrap and the world will beat a path to your door" is just not true. An NFP must get its message across if it is to thrive.

This requires good marketing, and good marketing is the result of good marketers. Many firms that were successful in previous time periods have failed in the new environment because of a lack of marketing know-how. If a firm does not have adequate marketing skills available within its own organization, its financial resources must be sufficient to acquire the marketing personnel.

Operations/Services Resources. Several distinctly different production resource elements affect a firm's ability to handle new opportunities—service capacity, cost structure, technology, and personnel skills. Capacity is influenced by previous commitments to acquire facilities. In the short run this capacity is usually fixed, but it can be altered, over time, for new strategic opportunities. The skills of personnel available during the short run are also considered fixed. Therefore a firm must have both the capacity and the skills on hand or it must have the financial ability to acquire them. The cost structure of a firm can be a determining factor for some opportunities. The ability or lack of ability to deliver services in a cost-efficient manner can determine an NFP's staying power. Technological capabilities must also be considered. Some new services may require technology not currently available in the company. If the technology cannot be acquired at a reasonable cost, some opportunities may have to be foregone.

Some appropriate equipment and space questions include the following. Are equipment and space adequate for present needs and for planned future needs? Are they in good operating condition? Are they costly to maintain or operate?

It is relatively easy to identify the strengths in each of these areas. When you attempt to define weaknesses, it becomes a little more painful. Often, organizations must call in outside consultants to be able to candidly pinpoint their limitations. But weaknesses and limitations must be recognized before you move on. The process should result in all the evaluations listed in the internal analysis being separated into strengths and weaknesses.

Often NFP planning groups identify strengths first and write them on a blackboard. Through discussions, the group agrees on perhaps five major strengths. They then have each person write two or three weaknesses of the organization down on paper, which are copied onto the board to generate discussion. Only with an objective appraisal of strengths and weaknesses can realistic objectives be set.

USING A SWOT ANALYSIS

The process of reviewing an NFP's internal operations for strengths and weaknesses and scanning the organization's external environment for opportunities is called a SWOT analysis. As was noted in Chapter 2, SWOT is an acronym for *S*trengths, *W*eaknesses, *O*pportunities, and *T*hreats.

The ultimate goal of a SWOT analysis, on the one hand, is to match vital operational strengths with major environmental opportunities. On the other, a SWOT analysis provides a basis for improving our weaknesses or at least minimizing them and avoiding or managing environmental threats to our operations. Ideally, a SWOT study helps identify a distinctive competence that can be used to tap an important opportunity in our NFP's environment allowing us to effectively fulfill our strategic objectives and our ongoing mission as an organization.

Exhibit 4-1 illustrates one format for evaluating internal strengths and weaknesses in light of external opportunities by taking into consideration the application of major organizational resources. Each factor–capacity, personnel, marketing, finance, and management–is rated in relation to an opportunity on a quantitative basis.

An alternate approach is to analyze these resources in relation to the opportunity as a strength or weakness. This approach is shown in Exhibit 4-2. For each strength and weakness identified, strategy implications are drawn.

Analysis of strengths and weaknesses flows logically from the identification of the resources relative to the opportunity. Each resource, when evaluated within this framework, can be labeled as a strength or weakness, and the implications of that strength or weakness for a specific opportunity can be evaluated.

MAKING ASSUMPTIONS

The next step is to make your major assumptions. These should be made about spheres over which you have little or absolutely no control, e.g., the external environment. One good place to start is to extend some of the items studied in the external analysis.

Using the environmental trends for an NFP hospital noted earlier, assumptions for planning and management of the hospital might well include such statements as those listed below:

EXHIBIT 4-1. NFP Organization Resource Evaluation Matrix

	Rating				
	Very Good (1)	Good (2)	Fair (3)	Poor (4)	Very Poor (5)
Operations/Services					
Production Capacity	___	___	___	___	___
Cost Structure	___	___	___	___	___
Technology	___	___	___	___	___
Personnel Skills	___	___	___	___	___
Production	___	___	___	___	___
Operations Score	___	___	___	___	___
Marketing					
Marketing Skills	___	___	___	___	___
Facilities	___	___	___	___	___
Location	___	___	___	___	___
Marketing Score	___	___	___	___	___
Finance					
Fixed Capital Requirements	___	___	___	___	___
Working Capital Requirements	___	___	___	___	___
Finance score	___	___	___	___	___
Managerial					
Number	___	___	___	___	___
Depth	___	___	___	___	___
Experience	___	___	___	___	___
Managerial Score	___	___	___	___	___
Total Score	___	___	___	___	___

Source: Adapted from Stewart H. Rewoldt, James R. Scott, and Martin R. Warshaw. *Introduction to Marketing Management* (Homewood, IL: Richard D. Irwin, Inc., 1977), pp. 257, 261.

EXHIBIT 4-2. Analysis of Strengths and Weaknesses

Factor	Opportunity Implication
A. Marketing resources	
1. Strengths:	
Established facilities	New service could use the same facilities
2. Weaknesses:	
No in-house advertising	Service needs strong advertising effort and dependence on ad agency
B. Financial resources	
1. Strengths:	
Good cash position and strong earnings record	Continue current sponsor support plans
2. Weaknesses:	
Higher than average debt/asset ratio	Must fund through internal sources
C. Service capacity	
1. Strengths:	
High quality operations	Go for quality end of market
2. Weaknesses:	
Low volunteer availability	Restricts service availability
D. Managerial resources	
1. Strengths:	
Strong planning, effective staff	Cost-effectiveness in operation
2. Weaknesses:	
No experience with new service	Hire new assistant

1. Intervention by the federal government in health care delivery will continue to escalate. Some form of national health insurance will be mandated by Congress within five years.
2. Federal reimbursement for health care will continue to drop and philanthropy will largely be a thing of the past.
3. Employers will take an increasingly aggressive stance as health care purchasers in trying to control the costs of health care benefits for their employees.
4. Technological advances will continue at an ever-increasing pace. Many will continue to be expensive, but others will represent competition to traditional in-house services as more over-the-counter tests are approved for direct public use.

A list should be developed of certain assumptions that characterize strategic aspects of your NFP's operation. Assumptions are those situational trends which in our estimate will significantly impact our NFP's activities during the period being planned for. Major considerations include the nature of our clients' expectations, our funding sources, and our competitors. Although these assumptions are outside our control, they are basic beginning points for the NFP's plans for future delivery of services.

Here are some assumptions that fit the strategic planning model.

1. Quality leads to quantity. The quality of service leads to expansion of services. Higher quality of services leads to greater demand for services.
2. A commitment to excellence produces confidence in the NFP's leadership and administration. If the administration is committed to excellence and demonstrates it in its leadership style, then the staff and volunteers will feed off this confidence allowing them to persevere in uncertain situations.
3. Sponsorship and funding of the NFP will continue to be a challenge, but continued effort will produce sources of funds, sometimes from new and unexpected directions.
4. Each service offered has some unique aspects to it that may require new ways of doing things. Policies and procedures should be adapted to produce the best results, not just standardization.
5. Improving the efficiency of your NFP's operations should not

be such an overwhelming focus that staff and volunteers lose sight of the inherent good to society the NFP seeks to provide.

Assumptions must be directly related to action. Note the relationship between assumption and proposed action in the following example:

Assumption: The number of nurses needed to staff hospital units will be difficult to recruit due to changing demographics in relation to our hospital's location.

For an inner city NFP hospital, an effective environmental analysis translates into a thorough look at what is going on in its service area. In this case, an important trend might indicate that most nurses have moved to the suburbs and prefer to work in hospitals near home rather than commute to the inner city. The assumption that this will continue to be the case provides the basis for a plan of action to deal with the long-term staffing problems this will cause.

Action: Open your own nursing school and recruit students from surrounding neighborhoods.

People leave the inner city for reasons, many of which are economic. Those that remain often have little hope of improving their living standards. Inner city careers which pay good wages are rare. An inner city NFP that develops its own nursing school could meet the neighborhood's needs for good jobs as well as the hospital's needs for competent nurses. Importantly, the school develops local talent who may be more likely to stay with the hospital for the long haul. Thus, both the hospital's and the neighborhood's problems are relieved.

The key is knowing what is going on and being alert to opportunities. Then develop a full plan based on a few assumptions. If an assumption changes, the plan changes.

The worksheet at the end of this chapter and in Section III of Appendix A is a useful tool for internal and external analysis. Answering all the questions can be a good start in assessing the organization in several areas.

SUMMARY

This chapter has emphasized the importance of coming to grips with the external and internal environments in which you must work to fulfill your mission. Minimizing weaknesses and capitalizing on strengths helps bolster the ability of an organization to operate in its external environment. Specifying the assumptions provides a basis for thoughtful consideration of the basic premises on which you operate. They should also cause you to ponder the "What if, What then" scenarios that help avoid disruptions in the organization's operations through contingency planning.

SITUATION ANALYSIS AND ASSUMPTIONS WORKSHEET

This worksheet will aid you in completing a *S*trengths, *W*eaknesses, *O*pportunities, and *T*hreats (SWOT) analysis.

Step 1. **External Environment Analysis:** From industry surveys and your own sources of information, take your organization's pulse. You are looking for trends–what is going on now and how this relates to past trends that have influenced your NFP's performance. From this analysis, list key opportunities and threats for each of the following environmental sectors.

Government

Opportunities

1. _____
2. _____
3. _____

Threats

1. _____
2. _____
3. _____

Economy

Opportunities

1. _____
2. _____
3. _____

Threats

1. _____
2. _____
3. _____

Technology

Opportunities

1. _____
2. _____
3. _____

Threats

1. _____
2. _____
3. _____

Social Trends

Opportunities

1. _____
2. _____
3. _____

Threats

1. _____
2. _____
3. _____

Clients

Opportunities

1. _____
2. _____
3. _____

Threats

1. _____
2. _____
3. _____

Funding Sources/Sponsorship

Opportunities

1. _____
2. _____
3. _____

Threats

1. _____
2. _____
3. _____

Competing NFPs

Opportunities

1. _____
2. _____
3. _____

Threats

1. _____
2. _____
3. _____

Next, evaluate your external analysis:

Have you listed several international/national trends that affect your NFP?

_____
_____
_____

Have you listed several local trends that affect your NFP?

_____
_____
_____

Have you identified trends unique to your NFP (e.g., volunteerism)?

_____

_____

_____

Have you listed several of your most important competitors?

_____

_____

_____

Which are growing? _____

_____

Which are declining? _____

_____

What are the successful ones doing? _____

_____

Step 2. Internal Operations Analysis: Using the question guides below and your own information, list key strengths and weaknesses for each of the following sectors of your NFP's operations.

Management and Planning Systems

Use these questions to help you prepare your strengths and weaknesses list for this portion of your NFP's operation.

Do you have a planning system?

_____

_____

_____

How does it work?

_____

_____

_____

Is the organizational structure of your NFP allowing effective use of resources?

_____

_____

_____

Is control centralized or decentralized?

_____

_____

_____

Are performance measures and information system controls in evidence? What are they?

_____

_____

_____

What staffing needs do you have?

_____

_____

_____

Is there a motivation problem?

_____

_____

_____

Is your current strategy defined? Is it working?

_____

_____

_____

How efficient are operations?

_____

_____

_____

What is your synopsis of the current management situation?

_____

_____

_____

Now list your strengths and weaknesses for this section of your NFP's operations.

Strengths

_____

_____

_____

Weaknesses

_____

_____

_____

Financial Resources

Use these questions to help you prepare your strengths and weaknesses list for this portion of your NFP's operation.

What is your current financial situation?

_____

_____

_____

Do you have regular financial statements prepared?

_____

_____

_____

What tools would be beneficial in analysis?

_____

_____

_____

Do you have pro forma statements for revenue centers such as a bookstore, day care, etc.?

_____

_____

_____

Do you have a cash budget?

_____

_____

_____

Do you have a capital budget?

_____

_____

_____

Has a ratio analysis been prepared?

_____

_____

_____

Do you understand the time value of money?

_____

_____

_____

Do you understand and use break-even analysis?

_____

_____

_____

Have you analyzed current financial policies?

_____

_____

_____

Do you have cash policies?

_____

_____

_____

How are accounts receivable analyzed?

_____

_____

_____

How are accounts payable analyzed?

_____

_____

_____

Do you control inventory levels?

_____

_____

_____

Do you have a debt retirement plan?

_____

_____

_____

Give a synopsis of your current financial situation.

_____

_____

_____

Accounting analysis:

Depreciation procedures? _____

_____

Tax considerations? _____

_____

Decentralized/centralized operations? _____

_____

Responsibility accounting? _____

_____

Tools beneficial in analysis:

Do you have budgets (short- and long-range) established?

_____

_____

_____

Do you perform variance analysis comparing actual against planned performance?

_____

_____

_____

What costing methods are used?

_____

_____

_____

Do you do contribution margin analysis?

_____

_____

_____

Are there adequate controls, especially of cash, for each of your NFP's programs?

_____

_____

_____

What is your synopsis of the current accounting situation?

_____

_____

_____

Now list your strengths and weaknesses for this section of your NFP's operations.

Strengths

_____

_____

_____

Weaknesses

_____

_____

_____

Marketing Resources

Use these questions to help you prepare your strengths and weaknesses list for this portion of your NFP's operation.

Have you established marketing policies?

_____

_____

_____

Have you established what you will and will not do?

_____

_____

_____

Have you identified your clients?

_____

_____

_____

Have you identified your funding sponsors?

_____

_____

_____

What are your competitors' services and products, level of demand, and relative market positions?

_____

_____

_____

What are your distribution systems and location of facilities?

_____

_____

_____

What is the nature of funding and fees charged?

_____

_____

_____

What promotion (advertising sales promotion, and personal selling) activities are you using?

_____

_____

_____

What is your synopsis of the current marketing situation?

_____

_____

_____

Now list your strengths and weaknesses for this section of your NFP's operations.

Strengths

_____

_____

_____

Weaknesses

_____

_____

_____

Operations or Services Resources

What are your operations capacities?
What shape are your facilities in?

_____

_____

_____

What is the age and serviceability of your equipment?

_____

_____

_____

How automated are your operations?

_____

_____

_____

What are your transportation capabilities?

_____

_____

_____

Are safety programs adequate?

_____

_____

_____

How effective is your inventory control?

_____

_____

_____

Do you use quality control systems?

_____

_____

_____

Now list your strengths and weaknesses for this section of your NFP's operations.

Strengths

_____

_____

_____

Weaknesses

_____

_____

_____

Next, evaluate your internal analysis:

Active and inactive volunteer analysis?

_____

_____

_____

Average volunteer participation with various services?

_____

_____

_____

How many services rendered, clients served by type of program offered?

_____

_____

_____

Step 3: **Development of Assumptions:** List the major assumptions on which your plan is based.

1. _____

2. _____

3. _____

4. _____

5. _____

6. _____

Chapter 5

Establishing Organizational Objectives

Not failure but low aim is crime.

J. R. Lowell
American Writer

Management's job is not to see the company as it is . . . but as it can become.

John W. Teets
CEO, Greyhound Corp.

Some nonprofit people used to think that if you're doing good, somehow God will provide.

John R. Garrison
President, National Easter Seal Society

Goal conflicts may arise in any organization, but unresolved divergence of aims is likely to be more severe in not-for-profit enterprises.

William H. Newman
Professor of Business

When you are clear about your mission, corporate goals and operating objectives flow from it.

Frances Hesselbein
Former Executive Director, Girl Scouts of America

In this chapter we will discuss establishing objectives, the third step in the strategic planning process. After the purpose or mission of the not-for-profit has been defined, internal and external analysis completed, and assumptions made, then–and only then–can relevant objectives be considered.

Clearly, one cannot achieve goals if none exist. Although this idea is quite simple, many people overlook it. In order to accomplish anything, we must make up our minds to do it. If we fail to do this first step, we simply waste our time and energy by going in circles. Later, we look back at what we accomplished and wonder where the time went.

NATURE AND ROLE OF OBJECTIVES

The words key results, goals and targets are often used synonymously when talking about long- and short-term objectives. Whatever the label used, the idea is to focus on a specific set of target activities and outcomes to be accomplished. Think of the analogy of the archer used earlier. An NFP administrator wants his whole organization aimed at the same target just as an archer wants his arrow aimed at the bullseye. People get confused and disorganized if they do not know where they are going. The success or failure of a not-for-profit organization is based on its ability to set goals, as well as on tools with which to measure progress.

There are at least six reasons why NFP organizations fail to set clear objectives:

1. Many not-for-profit managers fear accountability
2. Many projects continue even when they no longer serve an organization's goals
3. Not-for-profits often undertake any activity for which money is available
4. Some not-for-profit managers fear hard-nosed evaluation may undermine humanitarian instincts
5. Not-for-profit managers must spend a great deal of time on activities that do not immediately further their goals (meeting with donors, fund raising, explaining programs, and so forth)

6. Not-for-profits have few, if any, financial report cards to tell them how they are doing.[1]

As objectives are established in the organization, some of those mentioned above may not be applicable. However, most of this list could be applied in any type of organizational setting.

Drucker states that "objectives are not fate; they are direction. They are not commands, but they are commitments. They do not determine the future, but they are the means by which the resources and energies of the operation can be mobilized for the making of the future."[2] Objectives can be defined as clear, concise written statements outlining what is to be accomplished in key areas in a certain time period, in objectively measurable terms. Objectives can be classified as routine, problem solving, innovative, team, personal, and budget performance.

Objectives can be set at upper organizational levels in key result areas such as growth, finances, physical resources, staff development and attitudes. They are also needed in sub-units, departments, or divisions of an organization. Most important, all organizational objectives must be consistent. Thus, a department's objectives should lead to accomplishing the overall organization's goals.

Objectives serve two fundamental purposes. First, they serve as a road map. Objectives are the results desired upon completion of the planning period. In the absence of objectives, no sense of direction can be attained in decision making. In planning, objectives answer one of the basic questions posed in the planning process: Where do we want to go? These objectives become the focal point for strategy decisions.

Another basic purpose served by objectives is in the evaluation of performance. The objectives in the strategic plan become the yardsticks used to evaluate performance. As will be pointed out later, it is impossible to evaluate performance without some standard by which results can be compared. The objectives become the standards for evaluating performance because they are the statement of results desired by the planner.

Objectives have sometimes been called the neglected area of management. In many situations there is a failure to set objectives, or the objectives which are set forth are unsound and therefore lose much of their effectiveness. To counteract this, a management tool called management by objectives (MBO) was developed. It emphasizes the need for setting objectives as a basic managerial process, providing coordination of activities at all levels of the organization.

For the NFP administrator, management by objectives translates into four basic steps.[3] First, the administrator sits down with each of his staff and mutually works out objectives that each staff member will pursue in his area of responsibility. These objectives should support the overall objectives established by the NFP. Each of the staff members with supervisory responsibilities, in turn, holds similar meetings with their staff or volunteers. These meetings should be held at each management level so that objectives are fully coordinated.

Second, in addition to objective setting at these meetings, strategies or descriptions of actions to be taken to accomplish each objective should be laid out. Third, follow-up meetings should be held periodically to monitor progress toward objectives, identify problems, and mutually determine methods to correct any difficulties. The final step involves an overall evaluation of goal accomplishment for individuals and units at year's end or the end of the planning period. From this, new objectives for the coming planning period can be determined.

ALTERNATIVES TO MANAGING BY OBJECTIVES

One way to be convinced of the usefulness and power of managing by objectives is to consider some of the alternatives.[4]

1. *Managing By Extrapolation (MBE)*–This approach relies on the principle "If it ain't broke, don't fix it." The basic idea is to keep on doing about the same things in about the same ways because what we are doing (1) works well enough and (2) has gotten us where we are. The basic assumption is that, for whatever reason, "Our act is together, so why worry? The future will take care of itself and things will work out all right."

2. *Managing By Crisis (MBC)*–This approach to administration is based upon the idea that the strength of any really good manager is solving problems. Since there are plenty of crises around–enough to keep everyone occupied–managers ought to focus their time and

energy on solving the most pressing problems of today. MBC is, essentially, reactive rather than proactive, and the events that occur dictate management decisions.

3. *Managing By Subjectives (MBS)*–The MBS approach occurs when no organization-wide consensus or clear-cut directives exist on which way to head and what to do. Each manager translates this to mean: do your best to accomplish what you think should be done. This is a "do your own thing the best way you know how" approach. This is also referred to as "the mystery approach." Managers are left on their own with no clear direction ever articulated by senior management.

4. *Managing By Hope (MBH)*–In this approach, decisions are predicated on the hope that they will work out and that good times are just around the corner. It is based on the belief that if you try hard enough and long enough, then things are bound to get better. Poor performance is attributed to unexpected events and the fact that decisions always have uncertainties and surprises. Much time, therefore, is spent hoping and wishing things will get better.

All four of these approaches represent "muddling through." Absent is any effort to calculate what effort is needed to influence where an organization is headed and what its activities should be to reach specific objectives. In contrast, managing by objectives is much more likely to achieve targeted results and have a sense of direction.

CHARACTERISTICS OF GOOD OBJECTIVES

For objectives to accomplish their purpose of providing direction and a standard for evaluation, they must possess certain characteristics. The more these attributes are possessed by a given objective, the more likely it will achieve its basic purpose. Sound objectives should have the following characteristics:

1. *Objectives should be clear and concise.* There should not be any room for misunderstanding what results are sought in a given objective. The use of long statements with words or phrases which may be defined or interpreted in different ways by different people should be avoided.

2. *Objectives should be in written form.* This helps solve two

problems: unclear, ineffective communication and altering unwritten objectives over time. First, everyone who has played the game of "gossip" realizes that oral statements can be unintentionally altered as they are communicated. Written statements avoid this problem and permit ease of communication. A second problem involves the tendency to want to "look good," often at the expense of actual performance. Unwritten objectives can be altered to fit current circumstances.

3. *Objectives should name specific results in key areas.* The key areas in which objectives are needed were identified earlier. Specific results, such as $100,000 in annual donations rather than a "high level of donations" or "an acceptable level of donations," should be used to avoid doubt about what result is sought.

4. *Objectives should be stated for a specific time period.* Objectives can be set for a short-run, more immediate time period such as six months to 1 year. Building on longer and longer time frames, accomplishment of short-term objectives should lead to successful completion of longer run objectives. The time period specified becomes a deadline for producing results and also sets up the final evaluation of the success of a strategy.

5. *Objectives should be stated in measurable terms.* Concepts which defy precise definition and qualification should be avoided. "Goodwill" is an example of a concept which is important, but which in itself is difficult to define and measure. If a planner felt goodwill was a concept which needed to be measured, a substitute measure or measures would have to be used. An objective related to goodwill which would be capable of quantification might be stated as follows: "To have at least 85 percent of our constituents rate our NFP as the best organization in the area in our annual survey." Phrases such as "improve volunteerism" not only are not clear or specific, but also are statements which cannot be measured. What does "improve" mean? Increase the number of volunteers five percent? By 40 percent? If the statement is quantified as "Increase the number of volunteers by ten percent by December 1," it can be objectively measured. The accomplishment or failure of such a stated objective can be readily evaluated.

6. *Objectives at each administrative level must be consistent with overall organizational objectives and purpose.* This idea has been

previously stated, but must be continually reemphasized because of the need for organizational unity.

7. *Objectives should be attainable, but of sufficient challenge to stimulate effort.* Two problems can be avoided if this characteristic is achieved. One is the avoidance of frustration produced by objectives which cannot be attained, or which cannot be attained within the specified time period. For instance, large percentage increases in the number of volunteer workers can be unrealistic as goals if an organization already has an unusually large volunteer program. The desirability and likelihood of substantial increases become doubtful.

The other problem is setting objectives which are so easy to attain that only minimum effort is needed. This results in performance evaluations that look good from a distance since every goal is being accomplished but, in reality, only camouflage lackluster performance well short of potential. Easy goals fail to maximize the contribution of a given strategic plan.

One approach to writing objectives which contain realistic, but challenging characteristics is to apply a set of criteria to each statement to increase the probability of good objectives. One such list follows:

1. *Relevance.* Are the objectives related to and supportive of the basic purpose of the organization?
2. *Practicality.* Do the objectives take into consideration obvious constraints (such as budgetary limitations)?
3. *Challenge.* Do the objectives provide a challenge?
4. *Measurability.* Are the objectives capable of some form of quantification, if only on an order of magnitude basis?
5. *Schedule.* Are the objectives so constituted that they can be time phased and monitored at interim points to ensure progress toward their attainment?
6. *Balance.* Do the objectives provide for a proportional emphasis on all activities and keep the strengths and weaknesses of the organization in proper balance?

Objectives that meet such criteria are much more likely to serve their intended purpose. The resulting statements can then serve as the directing force in the development of strategy. Consider the following examples of poorly stated objectives:

Poor: Our objective is to maximize volunteerism.

Remarks: How much is "maximum"? The statement is not subject to measurement. What criterion or yardstick will be used to determine if and when actual volunteer levels are equal to the maximum? In addition, no deadline is specified.

Better: Our objective is to achieve an average level of active volunteers of 100 per month within three years.

Poor: Our objective is to increase sponsor donations.

Remarks: How much? A one dollar increase will meet that objective but is that really the desired target?

Better: Our objective this calendar year is to increase donations from $300,000 to $350,000.

Poor: Our objective is to boost advertising expenditures by 15 percent.

Remarks: Advertising is an activity, not a result. The advertising objective should be stated in terms of what result the extra advertising is intended to produce.

Better: Our objective is to boost our number of volunteers by 10 percent in each of the next five years with the help of a 15 percent annual increase in advertising expenditures.

Poor: Our objective is to be the best NFP organization of its type in our area.

Remarks: Not specific enough; what measures of "best" are to be used? Number of clients served? Level of sponsor donations? Number of new programs started? Services offered? Number of volunteers or staff?

Better: We will strive to become the number one NFP organization of its kind in the metropolitan area in terms of the number of clients served within five years.

The following practical suggestions are offered for writing objectives:

1. Objectives should start with the word "to" followed by an action verb, since the achievement of an objective must come as a result of specific action.
2. Each objective should specify a single major result to be accomplished so the group will know precisely when the objective has been achieved.
3. An objective should have a target date for accomplishment.
4. The objective should relate directly to the mission statement of the group or individual. A local chapter of a national charity should not write an objective outside the scope of its own mission statement or one that pertains more to the mission statement of the parent organization. This may seem obvious, but groups often commit themselves to projects for which they have neither responsibility nor authority.
5. The objective must be understandable to those who will be working to achieve the specified results.
6. It must be possible to achieve.
7. It should be consistent with parent organization policies and practices.

TYPES OF OBJECTIVES INCLUDED IN A STRATEGIC PLAN

Strategic plans for not-for-profits usually focus on at least four types of objectives: (1) services offered, (2) staffing and volunteers, (3) donations and funding, and (4) constituents. However, objectives should be established in *all* key result areas of the NFP's operations. Key result areas are those activities which are most likely to impact the performance of the organization. They are the few things that must go right if the NFP is to be effective and thrive. For most NFPs, objectives should be set for the following key result areas:

1. Level of staffing/volunteer participation
2. Level and sources of funds
3. Reputation and level of acceptance in service area

4. Clients served
5. Quantity of programs
6. Quality of programs
7. Leadership effectiveness
8. Quantity and quality of services.

Short-term objectives are stated for the operating period only, normally one year; whereas long-term objectives usually span five to twenty years. For example, five-year objectives can be set in areas such as clients served, programs offered, fund raising, services offered, and so forth.

In setting objectives, they are first stated in terms of what we want to accomplish, but as we develop the strategy we may discover that we cannot afford what we want. The available resources committed to a given program or service may not be sufficient to achieve a stated objective; and if the planning process is resource controlled, the objectives must be altered. It must be remembered that objectives are not fate, but they are direction. They are not commands, but they become commitments. As a planner, you must not fall into the trap of thinking that once objectives are set they cannot or should not be altered.

Here are some examples of key result area objectives.

Volunteerism Objectives

Levels of volunteerism objectives relate to an organization's influence in an area, and are a basic measure of the level of activity for a program or service. Volunteerism objectives are closely tied to scheduling of services, budgeting, and so on. Objectives for growth in volunteers may be stated numerically or as a percent of the total number. If the objectives are stated in percents, they also need to be converted to numbers for budgeting.

Examples of volunteerism objectives are given in Exhibit 5-1. Each of the objectives in Exhibit 5-1 is clear, concise, quantifiable, and stated within a given time period. The way objectives are stated must reflect what the organization can realistically expect to attain under a given plan.

EXHIBIT 5-1. Examples of Volunteerism-Oriented Objectives

1. Increase the average number of hours per month per volunteer from four hours to six hours this year.
2. Achieve an overall average number of 100 volunteers participating at least five hours per month within three years.

Funding Objectives

Funding and financial sponsorship are vital aspects of NFP operations, especially in an era where financial sources are drying up. While seeking funding should not be an end in itself, it is an inescapable fact of an NFP's life in order for it to deliver its services. The issue of continued survival offers a very practical reason for developing a specific statement about funding targets. Getting specific about desirable end results forces the planner to estimate the resources needed to underwrite specific programs and services.

A statement of whether resources will be available cannot be made without at least some analysis of the cost of providing services for activities which must break even. For new programs, the expenditures and contributions associated with the program should have been analyzed before introduction. For existing programs, donations can be analyzed to project continued levels of support. This information, combined with estimates of expenses involved in delivering services, provides a basis for statements of objectives about funding levels.

Sample statements are shown in Exhibit 5-2 as illustrations of funding objectives. The objective of a percentage increase in donations is the only one requiring additional information for its evaluation. The total previous funding would be required to determine whether this objective has been reached. Again, nebulous statements such as "acceptable donation levels" or "reasonable funding levels" should be avoided because of the possible variations in definition and the lack of quantifiability.

Keep in mind that the interactive processes of setting objectives and developing strategies must be used to set objectives that are realistic. The costs of many aspects of strategy cannot be estimated

EXHIBIT 5-2. Examples of Funding Objectives

---

1. Produce net donations of $180,000 by year five.
2. Generate a 20% increase in funding within five years.
3. Produce donations of $85,000 to support the homeless program within three years.

---

until a written statement of strategy is developed. If the strategy calls for a new program, for example, that strategy must be spelled out in detail before costs can be estimated.

Constituent Objectives

Constituent objectives may seem unusual to some, but their inclusion should be obvious. They serve as enabling objectives in volunteerism and funding. But fundamentally, they represent specific statements about the number and level of services the NFP will offer to its clients.

Constituent objectives are especially important in providing direction to the development of the strategy section of the plan. As shown in Exhibit 5-3 they specify results desired for constituents by program category. Client objectives should have the same characteristics as other objectives. They must be stated in objectively measurable terms and should be evaluated in relation to their accomplishment as a part of the monitoring and control system used in the plan.

USING ENVIRONMENTAL ANALYSIS DATA
TO SET OBJECTIVES

The objectives of a given plan are based on the data provided in the situation analysis discussed earlier. In other words, good objectives are based on a careful analysis of the external and internal environment of the NFP. A specific example of how data are used in setting objectives may help in understanding this point.

Consider a hypothetical child care agency in a city of approxi-

EXHIBIT 5-3. Examples of Constituent Objectives

---

1. Increase the number of meals served to the needy by 20 percent per year for each of the next three years.
2. Open at least one new shelter for the homeless within the next 12 months.

---

mately 400,000 with a desire to expand its services. In a search for opportunities for expansion, the agency has located a sizeable facility suitable for a wide range of activities which can be rented for a reasonable fee on a long-term basis. After some research, the agency believes it can obtain a government grant for funding youth programs. It also has learned through study that the total youth population has a healthy growth rate. Other environmental factors are, for the most part, also favorable.

In order to obtain the government grant, the agency tightens the focus of its environmental analysis. The effort identifies three market segments for youth services, one of which is for after-school activities. This proves to be a unique segment with special needs in terms of transportation, types of services and facilities desired, and timing of the events.

The number of youth was found in public records available through the school system, and the number interested in after-school programs was estimated through a telephone survey of a sample of 50 youth. The resulting analysis is shown in Exhibit 5-4.

Objectives derived through such a process represent the realities of the area and also the NFP's willingness and ability to commit itself to such objectives. This example should also reemphasize the logic in the strategic planning format. The analysis precedes setting objectives, because objectives must be based on realistic information that only a careful analysis can provide.

PERFORMANCE CONTRACTS

Objectives can become the basis of a performance contract for staff members. As an example, note how the objectives for an associate administrator can become a performance contract through the following process:

1. Properly written objectives submitted to the NFP administrator
2. Items discussed and negotiated with the administrator.
3. Objectives resubmitted to the administrator.
4. List approved by both parties (and perhaps the NFP's governing board).
5. In some organizations, both parties sign an objectives sheet.

PERIODIC REVIEW

One practical, easy way to record, communicate, measure, and update objectives is through a "Performance Plan Book" or "Management Plan Book." All objectives for the organization should be in this book. Objectives can be reviewed each quarter and updated. Shown below are examples of how objectives can be listed, kept track of, and presented for review. This process greatly reduces paperwork and provides a convenient method for review. Examples of how objectives might be set up in a management plan book are shown in Exhibits 5-5 to 5-7.

SUMMARY

Setting objectives is another major part of the strategic planning process. The necessity for objectives as well as their characteristics was presented here to lay the groundwork for identifying basic

EXHIBIT 5-4. Potential for After-School Youth Program

---

1. Population in metropolitan area = 400,000
2. Number of youth in metropolitan area (13-18 years old) = 37,200
3. Number of youth within agency's primary market area = 3,000
4. Percent of youth in telephone survey who say they are interested in after-school programs at agency = 10% (i.e., five out of 50 called)
5. Total number of youth who represent a viable target = 300 (i.e., 3,000 x .10)
6. Objective: Attract an average of 300 youths per week within three years.

EXHIBIT 5-5. Sample Management Plan Book
Overall Objectives, 1996-1998

	1996	1997	1998
CLIENTS SERVED			
Program One			
Program Two			
Program Three			
VOLUNTEER PARTICIPATION			
Program One			
Program Two			
Program Three			
Training Seminars			
FINANCIAL (per existing program)			
Average Donations			
New donors/Sponsors			
Budget			
Current Ratio			
Fixed Asset Turnover/Donations/Net Fixed Assets			
Total Asset Turnover/Donations/Total Assets			
Debt Ratio/Total Debt/Total Assets			
Debt/Total Funding			
Times Interest Earned/Donations/Interest			
STAFF			
Administrator			
Assistants			
BUILDINGS			
Build/Buy/Rent a New Facility			
Existing Facilities Improvement			
New Equipment			
Equipment Repair or Replacement			
EXISTING FACILITIES			
Systematic Safety Check			
Heating and Cooling			
Security: Burglar Alarms			
Lighting			
Parking			
Sound System/Other Special Systems			
STAFF/VOLUNTEER TRAINING AND MORALE			
Administrator Education Seminars			
Staff Training: In-House			
Staff Training: External Seminars			
Volunteer Training (per program)			
Yearly Attitude Survey			
PUBLIC RESPONSIBILITY			
Cooperative Funding Efforts With Other NFPs			
Facilities Sharing			

NEW PROGRAMS (per program)
Clientele Need Assessment
Competing Programs
Funding Sources
Funding Levels
Development/Start-Up Expenses
Operating Budgets
Paid Staff Required
Staffing: Volunteer Interest

EXHIBIT 5-6. Sample Review Sheet

MANAGEMENT PLAN, 1996

Objectives	Results
I. Routine: Set aside $5,000 for after-school programs throughout every month of 1996	On target
II. Budget Performance: Operate within the $50,000 agency budget throughout fiscal 1996.	On target
III. Problem Solving: Develop an efficient transportation routing schedule to be followed by bus driver volunteers by March 31, 1996	Met 90%
IV. Innovative: Devise a better layout for client parking during February 1996.	Done
V. Personal: Read the book, *Strategic Planning for Not-For-Profit Organizations*; attend communication course, fall of 1996.	Book completed; course registration mailed

EXHIBIT 5-7. Sample Objectives for an Administrator

ADMINISTRATOR'S OBJECTIVES, 1996

I. Routine Objectives

1. To make at least one funding sponsor visit per week.
2. To review each program's objectives and accomplishments by January 5, May 5, and August 5.
3. To attend the annual state administrators' meeting.

II. Problem-Solving Objectives

1. To develop a project for the 11- to 14-year-old youth to make a contribution to the community.
2. To develop staff training seminar by January 31.
3. To develop a set of criteria and measurable objectives for a volunteer retreat.
4. To hold a one-day open house for community education and volunteer recruitment within three months.

III. Innovative Objectives

1. To devise a better system of screening prospective paid staff.
2. To develop a method or methods to give all program leaders feedback on their budget performance. At least one method to be implemented by May 1, and another method implemented by June 1, 1998.

IV. Personal Objectives

1. To improve my understanding of the latest trends in service delivery; visit at least one similar NFP operation every six months.
2. To exercise four times per week.

V. Team Objectives

1. To work with the staff on revision and update of public relations brochure to be introduced in July.
2. To meet with the staff each Wednesday to troubleshoot problems and coordinate activities.

VI. Budget Objectives

1. To operate within the $100,000 yearly budget.
2. To retire 10 percent of the debt on the building.

types of objectives for such key result areas as clientele services, funding, and volunteer participation. The statements of objectives given as examples in this chapter possess the basic characteristics needed to serve both as a source of direction and in evaluation of the strategies developed in the plan.

REFERENCES

1. Harvey, Phil and J. Sander. "Charities Need a Bottom Line, Too," *Harvard Business Review* (January-February, 1987), Vol. 65, pp. 14-22.

2. Drucker, Peter. *The Practice of Management* (New York: Harper, 1954), p. 102.

3. Muczyk, J.P. and B.C. Reimann. "MBO as a Complement to Effective Leadership," *The Academy of Management Executive,* 3 (1989), pp. 131-138.

4. Adapted from Thompson, Arthur A., Jr., and A. J. Strickland, *Strategy Formulation and Implementation,* 3rd ed. (Plano, Texas: Business Publication, Inc., 1986), p. 52.

OBJECTIVES WORKSHEET

This worksheet will aid you developing objectives for your NFP's operations.

Answer These Questions First

1. What do your objectives need to relate to–clientele, services, funding, volunteer participation or all four? What about other key result areas? _____

   _____

2. What needs to happen for your program to be successful? In other words, how many people need to attend/watch, join, donate, volunteer, etc?

   _____

   _____

3. When do you want this to happen? By what specific date?

   _____

   _____

Now Write Your Objectives

Use the information in your answers above to write statements of your objectives for each key result area.

Objective 1: _____

_____

_____

Objective 2: _____

_____

_____

Objective 3: _____

_____

_____

Test Your Objectives

Now test each statement using the following criteria:

Is each statement relevant to the basic purpose of your organization?

1. _____
2. _____
3. _____

Is each statement practical?

1. _____
2. _____
3. _____

Does each statement provide a challenge?

1. _____
2. _____
3. _____

Is each stated in objectively measurable terms?

1. _____
2. _____
3. _____

Do you have a specific date for completion?

1. _____
2. _____
3. _____

Does each statement contribute to a balance of activities in line with your NFP's strengths and weaknesses?

1. _____
2. _____
3. _____

Chapter 6

Developing Strategy and Operational Plans

To mean well is nothing without to do well.

Plautus
Trinummus

If we can know where we are and something about how we got there, we might see where we are trending–and if the outcomes which lie naturally in our course are unacceptable, to make timely change.

Abraham Lincoln
American President

Just being able to conceive bold new strategies is not enough. The general manager must also be able to translate his or her strategic vision into concrete steps that "get things done."

Richard G. Hamermesh
Management Scholar

The best definitions of mission are operational. They lead to goals that tell people what to do and very often how to do it.

Peter Drucker
Management Expert

After developing a set of objectives for the time period covered by the strategic plan, the strategy necessary for accomplishing those objectives must be formulated. First, an overall strategy must be designed. Then the operating details of that strategy as it relates to providing services, promoting operations, determining location, and enlisting funding support must be planned to guide the NFP's efforts. This chapter introduces the concept of strategy and describes strategy elements and approaches to strategy development.

STRATEGY CONCEPTS

The word "strategy" has been used in a number of ways over the years and especially so in the context of business. As we discussed in Chapter 2, strategy means leadership and may be defined as the course of action taken by an organization to achieve its objectives.

It is a description first in general terms and then, in increasingly greater detail, of the activities the organization will undertake to meet its goals and fulfill its ongoing mission. Strategy is the catalyst or dynamic element of managing which enables a company to accomplish its objectives.

Strategy development is both a science and an art and is a product of both logic and creativity. The scientific aspect deals with assembling and allocating the resources necessary to achieve an organization's objectives with emphasis on matching organizational strengths with environmental opportunities, while working within cost and time constraints. The art of strategy is mainly concerned with the effective utilization of resources, including motivating people to make the strategy work, while being sensitive to the environmental forces which may affect the organization's performance and maintaining the ability to adapt the NFP to these changing conditions.

ALTERNATE STRATEGIES

Strategy options are the alternate courses of action evaluated by management before a commitment is made to a specific course of action eventually outlined in the strategic plan. Thus, strategy is the link between objectives and results.

There are two basic strategies an NFP can use to accomplish its objectives. These are a differentiation strategy and a focus strategy. In either case the strategy chosen must be an outgrowth of the organization's basic mission or purpose.

Differentiation Strategy

A differentiation strategy concentrates on developing and delivering products or services which stand out in the client's mind as distinct from other NFP's services. NFPs that pursue this strategy see that an important aspect of being able to fulfill their missions involves cultivating the perception of uniqueness in the minds of their service recipients and sponsors regarding the NFP's services or products. In a sense this means building "brand" loyalty so that when clients and sponsors think of a certain service their first thought includes the NFP.

For many NFPs, a differentiation strategy takes the form of several distinct services each targeted to meet specific needs of client groups in the NFP's service area. In addition to meeting more client needs, this portfolio approach to service development can be effective in generating increases in volunteer participation.

Various NFPs have successfully pursued a differentiation strategy. For instance, a local chapter of the American Red Cross provides an example of this strategy where a variety of programs are offered including:

Disaster Services–These programs provide emergency shelters for those displaced by natural catastrophes. Services include medical aid, food, and basic clothing for individuals in harm's way.

Health and Safety Services–Programs include first aid education, cardio-pulmonary resuscitation (CPR) instruction, water safety seminars, and AIDS information. Presentations are often made to schools and civic organizations.

Blood and Tissue Services–Services include outpatient blood transfusions, blood products storage, and mobile collection methods for blood donations. Bone and tissue programs provide products for transplantation.

By developing a reputation for high quality in programs such as these, an NFP like a local Red Cross chapter can come to be associated in a positive way with certain types of needs for a broad cross section of the community. Becoming synonymous with quality services in the public's mind can enhance financial sponsorship and volunteer participation. The end result of such differentiation is a greater capability to fulfill an NFP's mission mandate.

Focus Strategy

The other basic approach an NFP can use to pursue its objectives is a focus strategy. A focus strategy concentrates on a single service or category of very similar services which meet the needs of a specific group.

The Recreation Center for the Physically Limited (whose mission statement appeared earlier in Chapter 3) employs a focus strategy. The Center's services are highly specialized. It focuses on providing recreational activities as a means of enhancing the growth and well-being of its clients.

The Center's service recipients are tightly defined as well. Recreational opportunities are provided for the physically handicapped, excluding children under the age of five, within its service area. Using a focus strategy, the Recreation Center seeks to fill a service gap for the physically challenged in its community.

The main advantages of this strategy are: (1) it capitalizes on the distinctive competencies of the people involved, and (2) it concentrates on doing one thing well. These advantages can also create both a knowledge base of how to carry out certain types of programs, as well as improved efficiency in performing the services.

FACTORS INFLUENCING THE STRATEGY SELECTED

At least four factors influence the choice of a strategy selected by the organization: its internal resources, the distinctive competencies of leaders and members, the stage in its life cycle, and strategies used by other organizations. There is no one best strategy which will always prove successful. Instead, the strategy that is chosen must be the one that is best for the NFP, given the nature of these four factors. Resources, for example, may limit the organization to a focus strategy. The organization may even be an innovator in terms of ideas but not have the financial, communication, or personnel resources to offer other services.

As emphasized in Chapter 2, an NFP's strategy must be derived from its organizational purpose and objectives. If the organizational mission is focused on serving needs of diverse groups then the strategy used must be one that is compatible. In other words, what an organization *does* must be a function of what it *is*.

The distinctive competencies of the NFP have a direct bearing on the strategy selected. Distinctive skills and experience in dealing with the physically challenged, for example, can influence strategy choice. These distinctive competencies are the basis of doing things well.

The organization's life cycle stage is an additional factor influencing strategy selection. For example, an organization may begin with a focus strategy but add programs over time which serve more varied needs. Repositioning the organization through introducing new programs or serving new markets would be a pivotal point of the strategy.

The strategy selected must be given sufficient time to be implemented and affect groups served, but an obviously ineffective strategy should be changed. This concept should be understood without mention, but the resistance to change in many organizations is a common phenomenon.

OPERATIONAL PLANS

After all the steps have been taken and a strategy has been developed to meet your objectives and goals, it is time to develop an operational or action plan. The operational plan is the "action" or "doing" stage. Here you hire, fire, build, advertise, and so on. How many times has a group of people planned something, gotten enthusiastic and nothing happened? This is usually because they did not complete an operational or action plan to implement their strategy.

Operational plans need to be developed in all the areas that are used to support the overall strategy. These include operations, communication, finance, and staffing. Each of these more detailed plans is designed to spell out what needs to happen in a given area to implement the strategic plan.

The operations plan identifies exactly what services will be provided to a specific group and the exact nature of those services. For example, will it be food, clothing, shelter, job location assistance or a combination of these activities? If an NFP is trying to launch a service in an urban area of low income people, the work could take many forms. It could be a "satellite" program, a literacy program, or concentrate on housing and feeding the homeless. These, of course, are completely different types of activities and must be carefully planned. The communication plan is used to communicate the nature of the program, location, and time to the intended audience and also to the rest of the NFP membership. This plan also needs to be well thought out and carefully analyzed to avoid a lack of communication or miscommunication.

For example, in developing their operational plans, a drug abuse program would need a communication strategy to provide information to people about their purpose and services. Its communication strategy could involve three key elements: informing, persuading, and reminding.

1. *Informing*–This involves providing information to individuals and groups about the organization. Specific elements of this plan call for:

   a. Use of video cassette presentations
   b. Newsletters, pamphlets
   c. Personal speaking appearances by leaders
   d. Hosting luncheons/dinners sponsored by supporters
   e. On-site visits by individuals/groups to headquarters or NFP service centers.

2. *Persuading*–This involves presenting the problems of drug abuse, principles for dealing with these problems, and how the NFP's services fulfill these principles.

   a. Prepare application forms with which service recipients may request additional information or interested individuals may apply as volunteers.

b. Provide convenient means for individuals to offer financial support or volunteer their time and services.

3. *Reminding*–This aspect of the strategy is to continue to provide information to people already familiar with the NFP so they will be constantly reminded of its work and needs.

a. Send letters/newsletters and other materials regularly.
b. Provide opportunities for volunteers to write supporters and future volunteers on a periodic basis.
c. Develop a complete file of individuals and organizations by name for future mailings.

The staffing plan deals with identifying who will carry out the activities involved. Will it be the NFP's paid staff or volunteers? If paid staff are to be used, will they be full-time staff or part-time? Of course, if volunteers are to be used, they must be recruited, trained and supervised. Since many NFPs must rely on nonprofessionals to carry out plans, it may be necessary to develop a recruitment plan just to staff the activity.

Finances must also be planned. This is usually done in the form of a financial budget. The budget is the means to execute the plan. If the financial means to support the plan are not available you must adjust the objectives. There is a constant interplay between the budget and the plan.

Many people do not understand the budgeting process. The budget is a "tool." Too often, however, the budget becomes the tail wagging the dog for the NFP. "We budgeted it so we had better spend it," or "We had better add a little to this year's budget" are statements that reflect this misunderstanding.

Budget money must be tied directly to performance. Performance is measured against objectives. Key results and objectives in an NFP's operation need to be prioritized. Money and resources are then allocated.

An example of this interplay can be reflected in this hypothetical give and take regarding the operation of a homeless shelter. In a planning meeting, the NFP's leadership confronts the realization that most of their resources for the next two years would have to go into finishing current building programs. Only enough money was available to maintain the status quo of the job location program even though they wanted to expand it. That does not mean the job location program is not important–it is. But the timing for expansion and growth for the program cannot come until the other projects are completed.

Exhibits 6-1 and 6-2 are action plans for a large homeless shelter with several different types of services. The operational or action plans in this example are related directly to the strategy to be used and the objectives to be accomplished in a step by step fashion. This forces the planner to align objectives, strategies, and action plans together.

EXHIBIT 6-1. Action Plan

Action Plan: Job Placement

OBJECTIVE:
To have 150 homeless placed in jobs in the next five years (1994-1998).
 1994: 30 job placements
 1995: 45 job placements
 1996: 62 job placements
 1997: 95 job placements
 1998: 150 job placements

STRATEGIES:
 A. We plan to increase year by year as the shelter's sponsorship grows so that we will be able to place one-third to one-half of the shelter's service recipients.

 B. We plan to add one part-time paid staff member this year to coordinate placements.

ACTION PLAN	PERSON RESPONSIBLE	START DATE	DATE COMPLETED
The shelter director will search for a placement officer.			
Existing staff will orient person selected.			
Placement officer will set goals for number of organizations to be contacted to become part of placement network.			
Placement officer will train volunteers to assist.			

EXHIBIT 6-2. Action Plan

Action Plan: Meals Prepared

OBJECTIVE:
To prepare 500 hot meals per day, every day, served morning, noon, and evening.
   1994– 300
   1995– 350
   1996– 400
   1997– 450
   1998– 500

STRATEGIES:
   A. Develop broader range of food donors.
   B. Expand kitchen and seating facilities.
   C. Hire one additional paid cook.
   D. Recruit additional volunteer servers.

ACTION PLAN	PERSON RESPONSIBLE	START DATE	DATE COMPLETED
Seek donated architectural services for facility renovation and schedules.			
Make additional food donor contacts.			
Arrange for public services announcements for volunteers.			
Determine construction costs.			
Update training services for volunteers.			
Hire cook.			

Notice that the Action Plan format takes one objective out of a five-year strategic plan and isolates it for further study and analysis. In this case it shows the targets this homeless shelter is aiming toward with its job placement service and its meals preparation. Never go into action until the target is clear and understood by everyone. It is important that all those who execute these plans be in on the planning and be aware of what is going on. That is the key to enthusiasm and support by the people. With targets/objectives/goals in mind, the various strategies are agreed upon. They are listed immediately under the objectives. Next, all the "actions" that must take place must be listed. Also note that at the top of each section is a row to write in who is in charge, date started, and date completed. This document becomes not only a guide to action but a timeline for starting and completing plans.

The person or persons responsible and the expected date of completion must be agreed upon. Every person involved gets a copy of the plan with his/her areas of responsibility marked. Now one person can coordinate a multitude of projects and programs, because there is a clear record of what is to be done. As each action or task is completed, the person responsible sends in a completion report. The coordinator knows what is going on all the time with this approach.

Periodic updates of the action plan are carried out so that everyone sees the progress. After people become accustomed to using the Action Plan format, they discipline themselves. They do not want others to see that they are falling behind. This is a great time saving and coordination format. Appendix B presents sample strategic plans to illustrate the development of strategies to accomplish a mission.

SUMMARY

A well thought out plan supported by everyone succeeds. How many times do you see NFPs trying to do everything at once? The word "strategic" in the title of this book implies thinking, planning, and seeking order. All this can happen if an Action Plan coordinates and supports the overall plan.

STRATEGY DEVELOPMENT WORKSHEET

This worksheet is provided to help you develop a strategy for your not-for-profit organization.

Answer These Questions First

1. What are the distinctive competencies of your NFP? What do you do well that makes you different from other NFPs?

_____

_____

_____

2. What market segment or segments should you select to match your organization's skills and resources and constituents' needs in those segments?

_____

_____

_____

3. Do you have the skills/resources to pursue several segments or should you concentrate on one segment? Are the financial sponsorship and funding opportunities of that segment large enough to sustain your organization and allow for growth?

_____

_____

_____

Now Develop Your Positioning Statement

1. Distinctive Competencies _____

_____

_____

2. Client Segments Sought _____

_____

_____

3. Services Offered _____

_____

_____

4. Promotion Orientation _____

_____

_____

5. Financial Support Levels _____

_____

_____

6. Growth Orientation _____

_____

_____

Next develop your overall strategy (Growth, Stability, Retrenchment) for each major program:

Growth (add or expand spectrum of programs)

Growth: alternative strategy 1

Pros
1. _____
2. _____
3. _____

Cons
1. _____
2. _____
3. _____

Growth: alternative strategy 2
Pros
1. _____
2. _____
3. _____

Cons
1. _____
2. _____
3. _____

Stability (Keep same programs while improving on effectiveness and efficiency)

Stability: alternative strategy 1
Pros
1. _____
2. _____
3. _____

Cons
1. _____
2. _____
3. _____

Stability: alternative strategy 2
Pros
1. _____
2. _____
3. _____

Cons
1. _____
2. _____
3. _____

Retrenchment (major reduction or elimination in existing programs)

Retrenchment: alternative strategy 1
Pros
1. _____
2. _____
3. _____

Cons
1. _____
2. _____
3. _____

Retrenchment: alternative strategy 2
Pros
1. _____
2. _____
3. _____

Cons
1. _____
2. _____
3. _____

Recommended overall strategy for each program

Justification: explain why this is the best alternative
Pros
1. _____
2. _____
3. _____

Cons
1. _____
2. _____
3. _____

Finally, establish operational strategies for objectives in each key result area in each major program that supports your overall strategy for that program.

An action plan for each key result area should be developed. The action plan places objectives, strategies, and operational plans into perspective with each other and helps you develop the interrelationships among plans at each organizational level. It helps goals come to life with appropriate action.

ACTION PLAN

OBJECTIVE:

STRATEGIES:
   A.

B.

C.

D.

E.

Action Plan	Person Responsible	Date Started	Date Completed

Chapter 7

Evaluation and Control Procedures

It is a bad plan that admits no modification.

Publilius Syrus
Maxims

Nothing in progression can rest on its original plan.

Alexander Pope
English Poet

What gets measured gets done.

Mason Haire
Behavioral Scientist

[For non-profits,] precisely because the bottom line is not a measure of accomplishment, everything becomes a moral absolute.

Peter Drucker
Management Expert

. . . not-for-profit practitioners no longer have the luxury of measuring their successes by the volume of news clippings generated by press releases . . .

Sunshine Janda Overkamp
Senior Vice President, United Way of America

In non-profits, the volunteers have to feel they are accomplishing something. When you have a clear mission, people care . . . They "buy in."

Peter Drucker
Management Expert

The evaluation and control stage of the strategic planning process can be compared to setting out on a journey with a road map. The process includes identifying your destination (objective), determining the best route to your destination (strategy), and then departing for your trip (implementation of your strategy).

During the journey, you look for highway signs (feedback) to tell you if you are on the way to your objective. Signs along the way quickly reveal if you have made a wrong turn, and you can alter your course to get back on the right road. When you reach your destination, a new route (strategy) is needed to get you to new destinations.

Imagine what would happen if there were no road signs during your trip to let you know if you were on the right road. It might be too late to continue the trip by the time you realized you were traveling in the wrong direction. Yet many NFPs are involved in a similar situation, failing to analyze results to determine if objectives are being accomplished.

Failure to establish procedures to appraise and control the strategic plan can lead to less than optimal performance. Many organizations fail to understand the importance of establishing procedures to appraise and control the planning process. This chapter reviews the need for evaluation and control, explains what is to be controlled, and offers some control procedures. Evaluation and control should be a natural follow through in developing a plan as discussed in Chapter 2. No plan should be considered complete until controls are identified and the procedures for recording and transmitting control information to administrators of the plan are established.

INTEGRATION OF PLANNING AND CONTROL

Planning and control should be integral processes. In fact, planning was defined as a process that included establishing a system for feedback of results. This feedback reflects the organization's performance in reaching its objectives through implementation of the strategic plan. The relationship between planning and control is depicted in Exhibit 7-1.

The strategic planning process results in a strategic plan. This plan is implemented (activities are performed in the manner described in the plan) and results are produced. These results include such things as services rendered, donations received, and accompanying constituent attitudes, preferences, and behaviors. Information

EXHIBIT 7-1. The Planning and Control Process

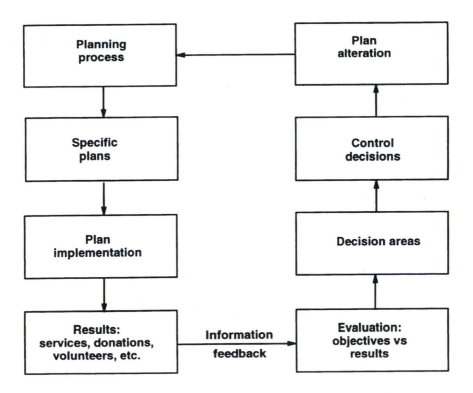

on these results and other key result areas is given to administrators, who compare the results with objectives to evaluate performance. This performance evaluation identifies the areas where decisions must be made to adjust activities, people, or finances. The actual decision making controls the plan by altering it to accomplish stated objectives, and a new cycle begins. The information flows are the key to a good control system.

The last stage of the strategic planning process, then, is to appraise the NFP and each of its entities to determine if all objectives have been met:

- Have the measurable objectives and goals been accomplished?
- How far did actual performance miss the mark?
- Did the attainment of the objectives and goals support the overall purpose?
- Has the environment changed enough to change the objectives and goals?
- Have additional weaknesses been revealed that will influence changing the objectives of the organization?
- Have additional strengths been added or your position improved sufficiently to influence the changing of your objectives?
- Has the NFP provided its members with organizational rewards, both extrinsic and intrinsic?
- Is there a feedback system to help members satisfy their high-level needs?

Timing of Information Flows

The strategic plan is supported by operational plans. We plan for the long run but must operate in the short run. If each of our operational plans is controlled properly, the strategic plans are more likely to be controlled. The administrator cannot afford to wait for the time period of a plan to pass before control information is available. The information must be available within a time frame that is long enough to allow results to accrue, but short enough to allow actions to align results with objectives.

Although some types of organizations may find weekly or bi-weekly results necessary, most organizations can adequately control operations with monthly or quarterly reports. Cumulative monthly or quarterly reports become annual reports, which in turn become the feedback needed to control the plan. Deciding what information is provided to which administrators in what time periods is the essence of a control system.

PERFORMANCE EVALUATION AND CONTROL

Performance should be evaluated in many areas to provide a complete analysis of what the results are and what caused them. Three key control areas are services rendered, donations, and constituents' attitudes. Objectives should have been established in all of these areas for the strategic plan.

Services Rendered Control

Control data should be developed on key aspects of the NFP's operations, especially as they relate to major service categories. An example of the type of performance reports needed is shown in Exhibit 7-2, where the number of volunteers needed for four service programs are displayed on a program-by-program basis. When such a format is used, the volunteerism objectives stated in the plan are broken down on a quarterly basis and become the standard against which actual volunteer participation results are compared. Number and percentage variations are calculated, because in some instances a small percentage can result in a large number variation.

EXHIBIT 7-2. Volunteer Performance Report
Quarter 1 (By Program)

Program	(A) Participation Objective	(B) Actual Participation	(C) (B–A) Variation	(D) (C ÷ A) % Variation	(E) (B ÷ A) Performance Index
A	100.	90.	−10.	−10.0	.90
B	95.	102.	+ 7.	+ 7.4	1.07
C	120.	92.	−28.	−23.0	.77
D	200.	203.	+ 3.	+ 1.5	1.02

A performance index can be calculated by dividing actual participation by the participation objective. Index numbers near 1.00 indicate that expected and actual performance are about equal. Numbers larger than 1.00 indicate above-expected performance, and numbers below 1.00 reveal below-expected performance. Index numbers are especially useful when a large number of programs are involved, because they enable administrators to identify those programs which need immediate attention.

Donation/Cost Controls

Several tools are available for establishing cost control procedures, including budgets, expense ratios and activity costs analysis. Budgets are a common tool used by many organizations for both planning and control. The budget is often established by using historical percentages of various expenses as a percent of revenues. Thus, once the total level of expected donations is established, expense items can be budgeted as a percent of total revenue.

If zero-based budgeting is used, where each period's budget is developed from scratch without benefit of last period's budget, the objectives to be accomplished must be specified and the expenditures necessary to accomplish these objectives estimated. The estimates are the budgeted expenses for the time period.

Donations or contributions are monitored by tracing gifts on a periodic basis, usually at least monthly. While many organizations have an annual drive for pledges, others are continually seeking contributions from constituents. A prerequisite to controlling contributions is an annual projection of operating expenses. This projection, broken down on a quarterly or monthly basis, becomes the standard from which deviations are analyzed.

For example, an NFP with a projected budget of $500,000 for the next fiscal year would be expecting about $125,000 per quarter, or $41,667 per month. If there are large variations related to certain times of the year, even the variations can be analyzed to determine the proportion of the budgeted amount received per month. If, historically, 20 percent of the budget were donated during December, then 20 percent of next year's budget becomes the expected level of donations to be used as the standard.

The same type of analysis used to control volunteer participation (shown in Exhibit 7-2) can be used to analyze data on revenues. This type of analysis should be performed on a timely basis to enable expansion or cutbacks of programs when revenue levels go above or below the expected amounts for the period.

Once the budget is established, expense variance analysis by line item or expenditure category is used to control costs. A typical procedure is to prepare monthly or quarterly budget reports showing the amount budgeted for the time period and the dollar and percentage variation from the budgeted amount, if any exists. Expenditure patterns which vary from the budgeted amounts are then analyzed to determine why the variations occurred.

Another control tool involves the use of financial ratios. The following ratios can be used to make comparisons against established objectives in each category, prior year's ratio performance, and typical ratios for the industry.[1]

Liquidity Ratios
>   Cash Ratio (cash and cash equivalents/current liabilities)
>   Current Ratio (Current assets/current liabilities)
>   Asset Ratio (current assets/total assets)

Contribution Ratio
>   Donation Ratio (total donations/total revenue)

Return Ratio
>   Return on Assets Ratio (total revenue/total assets)

Debt Ratio
>   Debt to Assets Ratio (total liabilities/total assets)

Operating Ratios

>   Net Operating Ratio (excess of income over expenses/ total revenue)
>   Fund Balance Reserve Ratio (total fund balance/total expenses)
>   Cash Reserve Ratio (total cash/total expenses)
>   Program Expense Ratio (total program expenses/total expenses)
>   Support Services Ratio (total support services expenses/ total expenses)

Other Measurements
Net Surplus or Deficiency (total income less total expenses)

Larger NFPs find revenue/expense centers a useful tool in control. For example, a drug awareness program generates revenues through the sale of educational tapes and incurs costs in recording, duplicating and mailing out tapes, plus overhead and labor costs. Tracking these revenues and expenses in a cost center would help control this service by letting the administrator know if it is operating at breakeven or if it is generating excess revenues which could lead to expanding the service, lowering the price of the tapes, or using the surplus for other services.

Constituent Feedback

The final area of performance evaluation is constituents, and involves analysis of awareness, knowledge, attitudes and behaviors of clients, volunteers, or supporters. Every organization should want its constituents to become aware of programs, services, or personnel; possess certain knowledge; and exhibit certain attitudes and behaviors. If these are specified, as they should be, in the objective statements, these objectives become the standards against which current constituent data can be compared.

Data on constituents must be collected on a regular basis. There are many ways to collect data, but annual surveys are commonly used. Constituent data are especially valuable if collected over a long period of time, because awareness levels, satisfaction, attitudes and behavior can be analyzed to reveal trends and areas for further investigation.

ESTABLISHING PROCEDURES

It should be pointed out that none of the performance evaluation data described are going to be available unless they are requested and funds are made available to finance them. Thus, data collecting and reporting procedures must be set up by the administrators who are going to use the control data in decision making.

The procedures will usually change over time as new types of analysis or reporting times are found to be better than others. The most important requirement is that the data meet the needs of administrators in taking corrective actions to control activities. With the expanded availability and use of computers by NFPs, much of the work can be computerized.

PERFORMANCE EVALUATION GUIDELINES

Several summary guidelines should be kept in mind when establishing an effective system for performance evaluation:

1. Performance evaluation must be self-evaluation.
2. Performance evaluation is for healthy, performing, growing individuals.
3. Evaluation should use both objective and subjective measures.
4. "No evaluation" is not an option.
5. When an evaluation process is perceived as legitimate, fair, and working, people will tend to use it responsibly. When it is not, people will still do something, but they may not feel the burden of responsibility.
6. Performance evaluation is a formal process (that is, it should be documented).

The control system in general should:

1. be linked to strategy.
2. be simple and economical to use.
3. measure both activities and results.
4. flag the exceptions.
5. focus on key success factors, not trivia.
6. be timely.
7. be flexible as strategy changes with environmental demands.
8. be reality-based where written reports are augmented by face-to-face follow-up (the idea behind MBWA–management by wandering around).

It is in the appraisal and control stage that NFPs really begin to see the benefits of the strategic concepts outlined in this book.

When people at all levels know the progress being made toward fulfilling the overall plan, it creates a sense of pride, accomplishment, and excitement. Strategic planning will not work well without a review of performance.

SUMMARY

No planning process should be considered complete until appraisal and control procedures have been established. Without such information, it is impossible to manage an NFP's activities with any sense of clarity about what is actually happening in the organization.

Performance evaluation is vital for control decisions. Information tells an administrator what has happened, and serves as the basis for any actions needed to control the activities of the organization toward predetermined objectives.

CONCLUSION

The thoughts we have offered throughout this book, we believe, will help make your NFP more effective. In the end, an organization thinking about instituting a strategic planning program should consider the following points:

1. The decision to implement this management philosophy should not be made in haste.
2. To the extent possible, it should receive management support.
3 It is strongly recommended that some type of training session take place in a neutral environment.
4. An outside resource person may be needed to get the program started.
5. When applicable, a person from the organization who can take over as the in-house expert should be assigned to work with the consultant.
6. Each organization must find the best way for its people to set objectives.

7. Each organization should come up with its own best method for handling feedback and reviews.
8. Be prepared to expose your management team to new ideas and new ways of approaching managerial problems.
9. Ways should be found to involve all employees in some decision making.
10. Personnel performance reviews must be conducted at regular, scheduled intervals.
11. Be prepared to spend time and hard work keeping the program viable, especially in the first six months.
12. Every organization and each of its decentralized entities can adapt MBO to its situation.
13. Goals must be negotiated rather than imposed unilaterally by management.
14. Periodic reviews of strategic plan progress are a must, and must be done by the boss.
15. Both extrinsic and intrinsic rewards must be obtainable by the individual and the group he or she works in.
16. Use methods for setting, reviewing, and updating MBO that require a minimum of paperwork.
17. If you start using MBO, begin benefiting from its use, and then stop, a big dropoff in morale will result.
18. Don't let a staff department dominate your program.
19. Involve volunteers in the planning process.

May your NFP's future be a bright one.

REFERENCE

1. Robinson, C. "A Study of the Financial Statement Ratios of ECFA Members: An Executive Overview," Paper presentation, University of San Francisco, (January 1990), pp. 2-3.

EVALUATION AND CONTROL WORKSHEET

This worksheet will aid you in developing tools to measure progress toward your NFP's objectives.

Answer The Following Questions

1. What kinds of information do you need to evaluate a program's or service's success?

   _____

   _____

   _____

2. Who should receive and review this information?

   _____

   _____

   _____

3. What time periods do you want to use to analyze the data? Weekly? Monthly?

   _____

   _____

   _____

   _____

4. What record keeping system do you need to devise to make sure the information you want is recorded for the time periods you specified in question 3?

   _____

   _____

   _____

   _____

Now Set Up Your Control Procedures

1. Specify the areas to be controlled:
   A. _____
   B. _____
   C. _____
   D. _____

2. Specify the format of the data for each area. (Is it to be numbers by month by program? Do you want number and percentage variations?)

A. _____

B. _____

C. _____

D. _____

3. Specify how the data are to be collected, who is to collect and analyze the data, and who is to receive the results of the analysis:

A. How will the data be collected? _____

_____

_____

B. Who has responsibility to collect and analyze the data?

_____

_____

C. Who is to receive which type of analysis?

Administrator	Types of Analysis
1. _____	1. _____
2. _____	2. _____
3. _____	3. _____
4. _____	4. _____

APPENDIXES

Appendix A:
Strategic Planning Worksheets
and Strategic Plan Outline

I.
PLANNING PROCESS WORKSHEET

This worksheet is provided to aid your not-for-profit organization in starting the strategic planning process. Use the answers to these questions to provide a foundation for completing the remaining worksheets.

1. Who should be involved in the planning process?

   _____
   _____
   _____

2. Where will planning sessions be held?

   _____
   _____
   _____

3. When will planning sessions be held?

   _____
   _____
   _____

4. What types of background material do participants need prior to starting the first session?

   _____
   _____
   _____

5. Who will lead the process? Who will ultimately be responsible for arranging sessions, and getting material typed, reproduced, and distributed?

_____

_____

_____

6. When and how will the staff, board, membership, or others be involved in the process?

_____

_____

_____

7. How will the results be communicated to everyone in the organization?

_____

_____

_____

8. Who will train/supervise staff members in working with their own staff and volunteers in setting objectives, developing action plans, and conducting performance appraisals?

_____

_____

_____

9. How frequently will the process be reviewed and by whom?

_____

_____

_____

10. Who will be responsible for dealing with external groups (sponsors, media, consultants) in preparing the plan?

_____

_____

_____

II.
MISSION STATEMENT WORKSHEET

This worksheet will aid you in writing a mission statement for your not-for-profit organization.

1. Write a statement for the following areas:

   Internal operations statement: _____
   _____
   _____
   _____

   External clientele statement: _____
   _____
   _____
   _____

   Needs served statement: _____
   _____
   _____
   _____

2. Now evaluate the statement.

   Does it define boundaries within which your not-for-profit will operate?
   _____
   _____
   _____

   Does it define the need(s) that your NFP is attempting to meet?
   _____
   _____
   _____

   Do you intend to have local, regional, national, or international scope?
   _____
   _____
   _____

Does it define the market (clientele) that your NFP is reaching?

_____

_____

_____

Has there been input from appropriate organizational members?

_____

_____

_____

Does it include the word "service," or a word with similar meaning?

_____

_____

_____

3. Next, submit it to others familiar with your organization to evaluate your statement of purpose and offer suggestions on improving the statement. In other words, does the statement say to others what you want it to say?

_____

_____

_____

III.
SITUATION ANALYSIS AND ASSUMPTIONS

This worksheet will aid you in completing a *S*trengths, *W*eaknesses, *O*pportunities, and *T*hreats (SWOT) analysis.

Step 1. ***External Environment Analysis:*** From industry surveys and your own sources of information, take your organization's pulse. You are looking for trends–what is going on now and how this relates to past trends that have influenced your NFP's performance. From this analysis, list key opportunities and threats for each of the following environmental sectors.

Government

Opportunities

1. _____
2. _____
3. _____

Threats

1. _____
2. _____
3. _____

Economy

Opportunities

1. _____
2. _____
3. _____

Threats

1. _____
2. _____
3. _____

Technology

Opportunities

1. _____
2. _____
3. _____

Threats

1. _____
2. _____
3. _____

Social Trends

Opportunities

1. _____
2. _____
3. _____

Threats

1. _____
2. _____
3. _____

Clients

Opportunities

1. _____
2. _____
3. _____

Threats

1. _____
2. _____
3. _____

Funding Sources/Sponsorship

Opportunities

1. _____
2. _____
3. _____

Threats

1. _____
2. _____
3. _____

Competing NFPs

Opportunities

1. _____
2. _____
3. _____

Threats

1. _____
2. _____
3. _____

Next, evaluate your external analysis:

Have you listed several international/national trends that affect your NFP?

_____

_____

_____

Have you listed several local trends that affect your NFP?

_____

_____

Have you identified trends unique to your NFP (e.g., volunteerism)?

_____

_____

_____

Have you listed several of your most important competitors?

_____

_____

Which are growing? _____

_____

Which are declining? _____

_____

What are the successful ones doing? _____

_____

Step 2. *Internal Operations Analysis:* Using the question guides below and your own information, list key strengths and weaknesses for each of the following sectors of your NFP's operations.

Management and Planning Systems

Use these questions to help you prepare your strengths and weaknesses list for this portion of your NFP's operation.

Do you have a planning system?

_____

_____

How does it work?

_____

_____

Is the organizational structure of your NFP allowing effective use of resources?

_____

_____

Is control centralized or decentralized?

_____

_____

Are performance measures and information system controls in evidence? What are they?

_____

_____

_____

What staffing needs do you have?

_____

_____

_____

Is there a motivation problem?

_____

_____

_____

Is your current strategy defined? Is it working?

_____

_____

_____

How efficient are operations?

_____

_____

_____

What is your synopsis of the current management situation?

_____

_____

_____

Now list your strengths and weaknesses for this section of your NFP's operations.

Strengths

_____

_____

_____

Weaknesses

_____

_____

_____

Financial Resources

Use these questions to help you prepare your strengths and weaknesses list for this portion of your NFP's operation.

What is your current financial situation?

_____

_____

_____

Do you have regular financial statements prepared?

_____

_____

_____

What tools would be beneficial in analysis?

_____

_____

_____

Do you have pro forma statements for revenue centers such as a bookstore, daycare, etc.?

_____

_____

_____

Do you have a cash budget?

_____

_____

_____

Do you have a capital budget?

_____

_____

_____

Has a ratio analysis been prepared?

_____

_____

_____

Do you understand the time value of money?

_____

_____

_____

Do you understand and use break-even analysis?

_____

_____

_____

Have you analyzed current financial policies?

_____

_____

_____

Do you have cash policies?

_____

_____

_____

How are accounts receivable analyzed?

_____

_____

_____

How are accounts payable analyzed?

_____

_____

_____

Do you control inventory levels?

_____

_____

_____

Do you have a debt retirement plan?

_____

_____

_____

Give a synopsis of your current financial situation.

_____

_____

_____

Accounting analysis:

   Depreciation procedures? _____

   _____

   Tax considerations? _____

   _____

   Decentralized/centralized operations? _____

   _____

   Responsibility accounting? _____

   _____

Tools beneficial in analysis:

   Do you have budgets (short- and long-range) established?

   _____

   _____

   _____

   Do you perform variance analysis comparing actual against planned performance?

   _____

   _____

   _____

   What costing methods are used?

   _____

   _____

   _____

   Do you do contribution margin analysis?

   _____

   _____

   _____

   Are there adequate controls, especially of cash, for each of your NFP's programs?

   _____

   _____

   _____

What is your synopsis of the current accounting situation?

_____

_____

_____

Now list your strengths and weaknesses for this section of your NFP's operations.

Strengths

_____

_____

_____

Weaknesses

_____

_____

_____

Marketing Resources

Use these questions to help you prepare your strengths and weaknesses list for this portion of your NFP's operation.

Have you established marketing policies?

_____

_____

_____

Have you established what you will and will not do?

_____

_____

_____

Have you identified your clients?

_____

_____

_____

Have you identified your funding sponsors?

_____

_____

_____

What are your competitors' services and products, level of demand, and relative market positions?

_____

_____

_____

What are your distribution systems and location of facilities?

_____

_____

_____

What is the nature of funding and fees charged?

_____

_____

_____

What promotion (advertising sales promotion, and personal selling) activities are you using?

_____

_____

_____

What is your synopsis of the current marketing situation?

_____

_____

_____

Now list your strengths and weaknesses for this section of your NFP's operations.

Strengths

_____

_____

_____

Weaknesses

_____

_____

_____

Operations or Services Resources

What are your operations capacities?

_____

_____

_____

What shape are your facilities in?

_____

_____

_____

What is the age and serviceability of your equipment?

_____

_____

_____

How automated are your operations?

_____

_____

_____

Are safety programs adequate?

_____

_____

_____

How effective is your inventory control?

_____

_____

_____

Do you use quality control systems?

_____

_____

_____

Now list your strengths and weaknesses for this section of your NFP's operations.

Strengths

_____

_____

_____

Weaknesses

_____
_____
_____

Next, evaluate your internal analysis:

Active and inactive volunteer analysis?

_____
_____
_____

Average volunteer participation with various services?

_____
_____
_____

How many services rendered, clients served by type of program offered?

_____
_____
_____

Step 3: *Development of Assumptions:* List the major assumptions on which your plan is based.

1. _____
2. _____
3. _____
4. _____
5. _____

IV.
OBJECTIVES WORKSHEET

This worksheet will aid you developing objectives for your NFP's operations.

Answer These Questions First

1. What do your objectives need to relate to–clientele, services, funding, volunteer participation or all four? What about other key result areas? _____

   _____

2. What needs to happen for your program to be successful? In other words, how many people need to attend/watch, join, donate, volunteer, etc?

   _____

   _____

3. When do you want this to happen? By what specific date?

   _____

   _____

Now Write Your Objectives

Use the information in your answers above to write statements of your objectives for each key result area.

Objective 1: _____

_____

_____

Objective 2: _____

_____

_____

Objective 3: _____

_____

_____

Test Your Objectives

Now test each statement using the following criteria:

Is each statement relevant to the basic purpose of your organization?
1. _____
2. _____
3. _____

Is each statement practical?
1. _____
2. _____
3. _____

Does each statement provide a challenge?
1. _____
2. _____
3. _____

Is each stated in objectively measurable terms?
1. _____
2. _____
3. _____

Do you have a specific date for completion?
1. _____
2. _____
3. _____

Does each statement contribute to a balance of activities in line with your NFP's strengths and weaknesses?
1. _____
2. _____
3. _____

V.
STRATEGY DEVELOPMENT WORKSHEET

This worksheet is provided to help you develop a strategy for your not-for-profit organization.

Answer These Questions First

1. What are the distinctive competencies of your NFP? What do you do well that makes you different from other NFPs?

   _____

   _____

   _____

2. What market segment or segments should you select to match your organization's skills and resources and constituents' needs in those segments?

   _____

   _____

   _____

3. Do you have the skills/resources to pursue several segments or should you concentrate on one segment? Are the financial sponsorship and funding opportunities of that segment large enough to sustain your organization and allow for growth?

   _____

   _____

   _____

Now Develop Your Positioning Statement

1. Distinctive Competencies _____

   _____

   _____

2. Client Segments Sought _____

   _____

   _____

3   Services Offered _____

   _____

   _____

4. Promotion Orientation _____

    _____

    _____

5. Financial Support Levels _____

    _____

    _____

6. Growth Orientation _____

    _____

    _____

*Next develop your overall strategy (Growth, Stability, Retrench-
ment) for each major program:*

Growth (add or expand spectrum of programs)

Growth: alternative strategy 1

Pros
1. _____
2. _____
3. _____

Cons
1. _____
2. _____
3. _____

Growth: alternative strategy 2

Pros
1. _____
2. _____
3. _____

Cons
1. _____
2. _____
3. _____

Stability (Keep same programs while improving on effectiveness and efficiency)

Stability: alternative strategy 1

Pros
1. _____
2. _____
3. _____

Cons
1. _____
2. _____
3. _____

Stability: alternative strategy 2

Pros
1. _____
2. _____
3. _____

Cons
1. _____
2. _____
3. _____

Retrenchment (major reduction or elimination in existing programs)

Retrenchment: alternative strategy 1

Pros
1. _____
2. _____
3. _____

Cons
1. _____
2. _____
3. _____

Retrenchment: alternative strategy 2

Pros

1. _____
2. _____
3. _____

Cons

1. _____
2. _____
3. _____

Recommended overall strategy for each program

Justification: explain why this is the best alternative

Pros

1. _____
2. _____
3. _____

Cons

1. _____
2. _____
3. _____

Finally, establish operational strategies for objectives in each key result area in each major program that supports your overall strategy for that program.

An action plan for each key result area should be developed. The action plan places objectives, strategies, and operational plans into perspective with each other and helps you develop the interrelationships among plans at each organizational level. It helps goals come to life with appropriate action.

ACTION PLAN

OBJECTIVE:

STRATEGIES:

    A.

    B.

    C.

    D.

    E.

Action Plan	Person Responsible	Date Started	Date Completed

VI.
EVALUATION AND CONTROL WORKSHEET

This worksheet will aid you in developing tools to measure progress toward your NFP's objectives.

Answer the Following Questions

1. What kinds of information do you need to evaluate a program's or service's success? _____

   _____

   _____

2. Who should receive and review this information?

   _____

   _____

   _____

3. What time periods do you want to use to analyze the data? Weekly? Monthly?

   _____

   _____

   _____

4. What record keeping system do you need to devise to make sure the information you want is recorded for the time periods you specified in question 3?

   _____

   _____

   _____

Now Set Up Your Control Procedures

1. Specify the areas to be controlled:
   A. _____
   B. _____
   C. _____
   D. _____

2. Specify the format of the data for each area. (Is it to be numbers by month by program? Do you want number and percentage variations?)

    A. _____

    B. _____

    C. _____

    D. _____

3. Specify how the data are to be collected, who is to collect and analyze the data, and who is to receive the results of the analysis:

    A. How will the data be collected? _____

    _____

    _____

    B. Who has responsibility to collect and analyze the data?

    _____

    _____

    C. Who is to receive which type of analysis?

Administrator	Types of Analysis
1. _____	1. _____
2. _____	2. _____
3. _____	3. _____
4. _____	4. _____

VII.
STRATEGIC PLAN OUTLINE

Using the information developed with the strategic planning worksheets, your strategic plan can be compiled. Plan descriptions can take many forms. (Note sample plans.) One useful approach is captured in the following outline.

Strategic Plan

I. Executive Summary
    * Highlights of each of the following plan sections (1-2 pages)

II. Mission Statement

III. Overview of Overall Strategies and Strategic Objectives
    1. Description of major challenges and problems facing the NFP.
    2. Description of major assumptions on which the strategic plan is based.
    3. Summary of major objectives and overall strategies as they relate to mission and challenges noted describe how major strategies:
        a. capitalize on distinctive competence and key strengths
        b. manage around or improve on major weaknesses
        c. overcome major external threats
        d. tap key opportunities
        e. fulfill mission

III. Strategic Plan Implementation: Operational Objectives and Strategies by Program or Service
    1. Program 1
        a. Key results area 1
            1. major objective 1
                *strategy 1 description to achieve major objective 1
                *strategy 2 description to achieve major objective 1
                *evaluation and control standards and time frames

2. major objective 2
   * strategy 1 description to achieve major objective 2
   * strategy 2 description to achieve major objective 2
   * evaluation and control standards and time frames
b. Key result area 2
   1. major objective 1
      * strategy 1 description to achieve major objective 1
      * strategy 2 description to achieve major objective 1
      * evaluation and control standards and time frames
   2. major objective 2
      * strategy 1 description to achieve major objective 2
      * strategy 2 description to achieve major objective 2
      *evaluation and control standards and time frames
2. Program 2
   a. Key result area 1
      1. major objective 1
         * strategy 1 description to achieve major objective 1
         * strategy 2 description to achieve major objective 1
         * evaluation and control standards and time frames
      2. major objective 2
         * strategy 1 description to achieve major objective 2
         * strategy 2 description to achieve major objective 2
         * evaluation and control standards and time frames
   b. Key result area 2
      1. major objective 1
         * strategy 1 description to achieve major objective 1
         * strategy 2 description to achieve major objective 1
         * evaluation and control standards and time frames
      2. major objective 2
         * strategy 1 description to achieve major objective 2
         * strategy 2 description to achieve major objective 2
         * evaluation and control standards and time frames

IV. Summary and Conclusion
   *Highlights of plan's key points showing how they successfully deal with major issues and problems of the NFP and fulfill ongoing mission.

Appendix B:
Sample Strategic Plans

STRATEGIC PLAN FOR A LOCAL CHAPTER
OF THE AMERICAN RED CROSS

SECTION I: Purpose

A. Purpose Statement

The mission of the American Red Cross is to improve the quality of human life, to enhance self-reliance and concern for others; and to help people avoid, prepare for and cope with emergencies. It does this through services that are governed and directed by volunteers and are consistent with its congressional charter and the principles of the International Red Cross.

Locally, the purpose of the Metro Area Chapter/State Regional Blood Services of the Red Cross is to meet the basic human needs of the community by providing medical, social, psychological and moral support, to alleviate suffering and to improve the quality of human life, during times of disaster, by using quality and timely relief services. This is accomplished through public support and the combined resources of career staff and volunteers consistent with the mission of the American Red Cross and in partnership with the Metro Area United Way.

B. Purpose Statement Analysis

A purpose statement for any organization must answer the following questions:

1. What is the business you are in?
2. What is the scope of the organization?

3. Is the need satisfied in the marketplace?
4. Who are your customers?
5. Is your organization profit or not-for-profit?
6. What is your ethics statement?

In response to these questions the Metro Area Chapter of the American Red Cross offers the following answers.

1. The American Red Cross is an emergency service organization. Emergencies can range from unpredictable disasters, such as tornados and floods, to predictable situations, such as blood and tissue needs and aid to the homeless.
2. The scope of the organization is primarily the Metro area (Metro Area Chapter) and northwestern area of the state (State Regional Blood Services). The organization works directly with the American Red Cross and, in turn, with the International Red Cross.
3. A congressional order has insured that the needs of the marketplace are met. The Red Cross has and will continue to meet the ever changing needs of its community.
4. Red Cross Services are available to anyone in need.
5. The organization is not-for-profit.
6. The mission of the Red Cross states its intent to improve and enhance the quality of human life by alleviating suffering. It accomplishes this goal without regard to race, creed, or religious affiliation and without discrimination. The Red Cross further assures that all funds received by the organization are utilized as designated to accomplish its mission.

SECTION II: Environmental Analysis

The environmental analysis stage involves looking at the past, identifying trends, and, in effect, taking the pulse of the environment in which the organization operates. There are changes occurring constantly in our society; and to keep up with these changes, the environment that a business or a service institution is in should be monitored constantly. The present environment must be studied so that the business can operate successfully in the future. The purpose of the environmental analysis stage in the strategic planning process is to give the organization managers a full understanding of what they are facing in the marketplace.

A. Industry Factors

1. The state's gross product (GSP), the measure of output in the state, will remain essentially unchanged this year. When inflation is taken into account the expected flatness in GSP suggests a real rate of decline of over 3.5 percent.
2. A large decline will occur in the oil and gas extraction component of the state's economy and in the building-related sectors of contract construction and finance, insurance, and real estate.
3. The impact of the depressed oil and natural gas prices will suppress drilling activity and push the number of jobs in the natural resource extraction industry down to totals that have not been seen for over 25 years.
4. Agricultural output is expected to increase modestly (2.2 percent) in the coming year.
5. Output in contract construction is forecast to fall.
6. The manufacturing sector of the economy will continue to suffer this year, although it will not be adversely affected across the board.
7. The transportation, communications, and public utility sector should show a moderate gain.
8. The overall economic downturn in the state has filtered down to the state's support industries. Output in wholesale and retail trade will grow slowly as individuals and businesses continue their conservative spending patterns.
9. There will likely be a slight increase in the average annual unemployment rate this year to 8.5 percent.

B. Economic Factors

1. Overall, last year's estimated decline in state employment in nonagricultural establishments was 26,000 workers. Unfortunately, further declines are projected for this year, with the loss of 18,500 jobs to the 1,135,000 level.

2. Oil and gas extraction in the state accounts for a large proportion of the expected decrease in state employment. Approximately 12,000 jobs were lost in this important sector in the state last year. This year, the losses are expected to be in the neighborhood of an additional 10,000 jobs.
3. The forecast is for a total manufacturing employment level of 158,000, a decrease of slightly over 1.0 percent compared to last year.
4. Little change is anticipated in wholesale and retail trade.
5. Transportation, communications, and public utilities, as well as personal and professional services, should register small increases.
6. The construction industry will lose about 3,600 jobs and state and local government will experience a decrease of about 6,000 workers, or 3.1 percent, to a level of 190,000.
8. *Metropolitan Area Employment Trends*

	Year 1	Year 2
Total labor force	332,700	344,300
Total employment	310,400	319,300
Agriculture	3,700	3,700
Nonagricultural	302,500	303,500
Manufacturing	40,100	41,500
Mining	21,100	20,400
Construction	15,000	13,600
Government	34,100	34,600
Services	69,100	69,500
Wholesale and retail trade	72,800	73,300
Unemployment rate (%)	6.7	7.3

C. Financial Factors

1. Last year all types of banks failed. Additional bank failures are expected this year, and the experience of last year indicates that the failures could occur in any bank category.
2. Last year third quarter losses also suggest the worst losses may still be ahead this year from real estate loans.
3. The trend for savings and loans suggests that financial distress should increase in this year as a result of worsening conditions in the real estate market.

D. Governmental Factors

1. The American Red Cross is mandated by Congress, it will therefore have full governmental support, especially in times of desperate need. Although the Red Cross is self-administrated and does not use Federal or State funds, it can count on assistance during times of need.
2. The State National Guard, police forces, relief agencies and other governmental agencies will work with the Red Cross at any time when the need exists. Hence, the Red Cross is well-supported by the government.
3. In times of national disaster, the President's declaration will channel enormous amounts of help to chapters in affected areas. The International Red Cross will also be supportive.

E. Competition Factors

Organizations Offering Similar Services (Metro)

First Aid–	American Heart Association Citizen CPR
	The Critical Link/Morton Comprehensive Health Service
Organs–	Body Donation
	State Department of Public Safety
Safety Education–	Metro City-County Civil Defense
	Fitness and Sport
	Hot Dots
	Metro Police Department
AIDS Information–	AIDS Speakers Bureau
	Shantil
	Metro AIDS Task Force
	Human Rights Task Force Metro Chapter
Disaster Aid–	Metro City-County Civil Defense
	Department of Stormwater Management
	Interfaith Disaster Relief Services
	United Neighbors Flood Metro Coalition
	Four Wheelers, Inc.
	Metro Baptist Association
	Metro Amateur Radio Club
	Flood Study Group

F. Social Factors

1. In times of major disaster, the Red Cross experiences overwhelming support from volunteers.
2. Churches, relief agencies, and the general public are always willing to donate time and money during times of need.

G. Demographic Factors

1. Through net migration, the state is expected to lose 46,000 people this year. The natural increase is estimated to be 23,000. On balance, the state population level this year is forecast to be 3,284,000 a 0.7 percent reduction.
2. *Metro Area Population Trends*

> Year 1–657,173
> Year 2–678,700
> Year 3–700,900
> Year 4–720,700
> Year 5–729,000
> Year 6–733,200

3. *Donor Summary*–by Chapters

Donations	Metro Chapter	All Chapters
1/yr	10,384 (58.8%)	24,653 (62.1%)
2/yr	3,983 (22.5%)	8,673 (21.8%)
3/yr	1,864 (10.5%)	3,706 (9.3%)
4/yr	864 (4.9%)	1,709 (4.3%)
5/yr	576 (3.3%)	981 (2.5%)
Total	17,671	39,722

Donations are made to the Metro Chapter an average of 1.7 times per donor per year.
Donations are made to all State Chapters an average of 1.6 times per donor per year.

H. Future Trends for the State

1. It is expected that the state's economy will bottom out this year, with next year projected to be a year of strong growth.

2. According to the State Economic Model forecast, the state's output as measured by real gross state product, will grow faster than GNP next year.
3. The forecast also shows substantial growth next year in the state's other major economic indicators.
4. A slowdown in the national economy is expected in the next two years, resulting in a setback for the state.
5. Employment in the state's nonagricultural industries is expected to climb by an average of 3.0 percent per year from the next four to eight years.
6. Within eight years, the state's real gross state product is expected to be 30 percent higher than last year's level.

SECTION III: Strengths and Weaknesses

Business organizations have certain strengths which make them uniquely adapted to carry out their tasks. Conversely, they have weaknesses which inhibit their abilities to fulfill their purposes. Managers who hope to accomplish their tasks are forced to evaluate the strengths and weaknesses of the organization.

The following strengths and weaknesses exist in the Metro Chapter of the American Red Cross and the State Regional Blood Services.

A. Administrative and Human Resources

1. Strengths

   a. In the Metro Area Chapter, volunteers constitute a large portion of the Red Cross work force. Presently there are approximately 150 paid employees and 500-700 volunteers. In times of need the volunteer supply is virtually inexhaustible.
   b. Volunteers, as well as paid staff, take enormous pride in their work.
   c. Because there is no formal sign-up process for volunteers, during disaster times the public at large can quickly respond to emergencies.
   d. There is a strong working relationship between management and the board.

    e. A strong public image is apparent in the organization.

    f. The Red Cross has an excellent volunteer and paid staff which is innovative and creative.

2. Weaknesses

    a. There is no established orientation and training program for volunteer staff.

    b. It is difficult to establish stability in the volunteer staff. It is also difficult to keep volunteer turnover low.

    c. The Red Cross has no comprehensive listing of their volunteers.

    d. There is an apparent need to better define the "charity" and "business" aspects of the Red Cross operation.

    e. The youth force is not adequately utilized by Red Cross.

    f. Generally, the staff is resistant to change within the structure of the organization. There is a concern that efforts to diversify have caused the Red Cross to drift away from traditional strengths.

    g. There is a general lack of board involvement.

    h. Rewards and recognition of volunteers and staff is inadequate.

    i. There is a lack of successful planning.

B. Financial

1. Strengths

    a. Excellent financial position. Good financial trend.

    b. Fund raising activities and programs are very active and there is an excellent response from the public.

    c. Solid financial base to enhance, which gives strong fund raising potential.

    d. Generally warm recognition of the symbol and wide community support for the organization as a whole leads to more contributions.

    e. Funding is solid and uninterrupted.

    f. The Metro ARC is able to borrow money against pledges coming in for the building fund.

2. Weaknesses

    a. Compared to United Blood Services, the Metro Chapter has a high level of national overhead.

b. Financial development results are not keeping pace with organizational needs.

c. The Metro ARC is not experiencing any income from an endowment fund.

d. Incoming funds greatly dependent on the success of the United Way Fund Drive.

3. Financial Ratios

a. *Unrestricted Liquidity*–evaluates the ability to meet unrestricted obligations from unrestricted assets.

$$\text{Ratio} : \frac{\text{Unrestricted assets}}{\text{Unrestricted liabilities}}$$

$$\text{Year 1–} \quad \frac{\$1,497,778}{\$273,859} = 5.469$$

$$\text{Year 2–} \quad \frac{\$1,032,837}{\$216,502} = 4.771$$

$$\text{Year 3–} \quad \frac{\$858,729}{\$228,807} = 3.753$$

b. *Operating Capital*–evaluates the ability to maintain current spending levels through the utilization of liquid assets–cash and investments.

$$\text{Ratio} : \frac{\text{Unrestricted cash + investments}}{\text{Total unrestricted expenses}} \times 360$$

$$\text{Year 1–} \quad \frac{\$21,064 + 0}{\$1,035,434} \times 360 = 7.324 \text{ days}$$

Expenses were unusually high in year 1 due to the opening of the new facility.

$$\text{Year 2-} \quad \frac{\$358,177 + 0}{\$903,147} \times 360 = 142.77 \text{ days}$$

$$\text{Year 3-} \quad \frac{\$196,836 + 0}{\$869,852} \times 360 = 80.635 \text{ days}$$

C. Equipment and Facilities

1. Strengths

   a. Superb, modern facility.
   b. State-of-the-art laboratory and equipment.
   c. Building well organized and departmentalized.
   d. Facility in a good location, which is easily accessible from the highway system.
   e. Recent addition of the downtown satellite is experiencing success.

2. Weaknesses

   a. Absorbing expansion areas of the new facility at a faster rate than planned for.
   b. Automotive maintenance costs are a little above normal.

D. Line of Services

1. Strengths

   a. High performance in service areas.
   b. Disaster services easily mobilized during times of need.
   c. Social support services are available to the public on a continuous, ongoing basis.
   d. Health and safety educational programs are especially strong in the areas of CPR and First Aid.
   e. Blood and Tissue services are the most diversified and well organized of the services offered by the Metro ARC.

2. Weaknesses

   a. Compared to other area blood services, the Red Cross carries high overhead and has a wide area for collection and distribution.

    b. Poor communication during disasters.

    c. Health and safety services in need of additional educational programs.

    d. Public unaware of the magnitude of social support services available.

SECTION IV: Assumptions

1. Metro economy, population growth, and unemployment situations will continue to change at the present rates for the next five years. More diversification in Metro industry is expected in the future which will improve Metro's economy and begin to decrease unemployment.
2. The need and competition for blood and tissue services will increase.
3. The Red Cross will continue its strong relationship with the United Way and will continue to be subsidized by the United Way and other organizations and individuals.
4. The incidence of AIDS in the Metro area will increase according to the national statistics and will have reached epidemic proportions in the next ten years.
5. Governmental and public agencies will become less involved with health issues, leaving the educational and maintenance needs to the Red Cross and like agencies.
6. Community awareness and support of the Red Cross will remain constant.
7. There will be a rising demand for Red Cross services.
8. Blood revenues are expected to expand and disaster-specific fund raising will be increasingly relied upon.
9. There will be a continued increase in costs due to the increased expense of modern technology.

SECTION V: Objectives and Strategies

    Some general objectives of the Metro Area Chapter are listed below:

- To aim towards being an organization supported mainly by volunteers to help people prepare for, avoid, and cope with emergency situations.

- To improve the effectiveness and performance of the staff and volunteers by strengthening communication, enhancing recruitment and assignment systems, and coordinating effective planning.
- To maintain and increase financial and community support from the Metro Area United Way, as well as other local institutions and individuals.
- To broaden the service network by researching new areas of human need, such as health maintenance education, tissue and organ donation, and AIDS prevention.

Specifically, the Metro Area Chapter of ARC will seek to accomplish the following objectives through the indicated operational strategies and tactics:

A. *Administrative and Management*

Objectives	Operational Strategies
1. By September this year, the Metro ARC will increase its financial support from all sources to provide quality servicesthat are responsive to human needs.	Expand funding techniques to include direct mailings. Pursue revenue generating avenues, such as events, grants, and contracts. Produce a one-minute commercial on cable network, which includes a toll-free number for donations. Donations could be charged on various major credit cards.
2. By December this year, recruit and retain career and volunteer staff to match jobs, programs and organization.	Establish task force to develop application/questionnaire design to pinpoint specific abilities of volunteers and potential employees.

Develop computerized log of these applicants, which will enable them to be retained, located, and utilized quickly and effectively.

Advertise in newspapers and PSAs about the ongoing volunteer recruitment drive.

3. This year, begin to increase board involvement in an effort to lower staff resistance to change by initiating increased two-way communication.

Have an employee meeting to explain the need for increased involvement from everyone and to outline the need for planning and organization.

Hold strategic planning sessions which involve board and staff.

Implement a two-way communication system between administration and staff, which includes an opportunity for input.

4. By next year, examine present building requirements and future needs, to determine when the present facility will be used at full capacity.

Before full capacity is reached, implement plans for expansion building program with target date.

Begin building fund-raising efforts one year before actual building will commence.

5. By March next year, increase youth volunteerism by 20% percent.

Strengthen school Red Cross youth clubs through increased visibility.

6. By September next year, implement a comprehensive volunteer training program.

Develop a volunteer training program in conjunction with volunteer recognition.

Establish levels of volunteer achievement to be attained and encourage volunteers to work up the ranks.

This action would result in recognition.

B. *Disaster Services*

Objectives	Operational Strategies

1. By June, increase contact with potential disaster relief shelters by 10 percent.

Plot existing shelters on map. Determine areas of need. Contact persons at potential new shelters to determine willingness to participate.

2. By August, assign sufficient medical staff volunteers and physicians to man disaster shelters.

Locate potential personnel in appropriate proximity to shelters. Train and log contact information to be used in the event of emergencies.

3. From August to November, contact and develop relationships with feeding establishments willing to donate food during disasters.

Poll feeding establishments and gather information on pledged amounts of food which could be obtained from each on short notice in the event of an emergency.

4. From November to January next year, establish a perpetual inventory of clothing, household accessories, etc. for individuals and families in need.

Contact establishments such as churches, retail stores, Salvation Army, etc. willing to donate these items.

5. By next year, increase communication capabilities during disaster by 50 percent.

Assign task force to design a plan for improving communication during disaster times.

Upon its completion, assign group to implement plan at each potential disaster location.

6. In two years, raise additional funds needed to equip newly acquired shelters.

Campaign for specific designation, one-time donations to fulfill the need.

During campaign, designate 5 percent of undersigned donations to aid in reaching this goal.

C. *Social Support Services*

Objectives	Operational Strategies

1. By March next year, increase moral, financial, and social support of governmental and nongovernmental agencies two-fold.

Actively involve the state National Guard in the plans and activities of the Metro ARC. First, by initiating meetings on a quarterly basis.

Increase the number of churches that will pledge their support to respond quickly and appropriately to emergencies within one hour.

2. Beginning September next year through June, increase corporate and private support of the ARC by increasing public awareness and appreciation of the organization's mandate.

Go to schools and colleges, at least monthly, to educate about the work and purpose of the ARC.

Increase the number of visits to private corporations, schools, and military facilities by the Blood Mobile Unit.

3. By December next year, the Red Cross will have a well organized network of financial and social support for the homebound or disabled elderly with a minimum of one visit per day.

Increasing the grass roots support of volunteers and finances from churches, institutions, and commercial enterprises to a sufficient level to support the project.

Collect food, clothing, and other living necessities from various individuals, schools, and other possible contributing avenues.

Offer in-home assistance activities for the elderly and other homebound by using social work majors doing internships at local universities.

4. By December next year, supplement various youth agencies by offering them

Acquire social knowledge and skill from various social workers for youth

better and more viable support.	leadership development centers, youth exchange programs, and other general youth programs.

D. *Health and Safety Services*

Objectives	Operational Strategies
1. Beginning January next year, Metro ARC will analyze what courses are being offered and their locations and by March next year will increase that number by 5 percent.	Examine the courses already offered. Analyze this schedule and broaden the number of topics to be taught. Contact and enlist instructors for these courses. Find new locations for these courses, preferably in areas not presently offering Red Cross instruction.
2. By December next year, Metro ARC will make the community more aware of the variety of Health and Safety courses offered, broadening the public awareness of the ARC as a whole by 50 percent.	Run newspaper ads for courses being offered. Contact high schools, middle schools, and hospitals about courses and provide them with course schedules.

E. *Blood and Tissue Services*

Objectives	Operational Strategies

1. By November, increase community awareness of blood tissue services by 15 percent.

   Contact various companies with regard to blood drives and tissue services. Set up booths at 5 new locations in area malls and other public places.

   Further develop the existing marketing strategies for bone and tissue programs, outpatient transfusion, plasmapheresis products, and blood production.

2. By January next year, the Metro ARC should collaborate with other providers of blood services based upon the interests of the community and current or potential customers of the ARC.

   Take a public relations posture towards area competitors in an effort to foster a cooperative spirit.

3. By June next year, the State Regional Blood Services should be able to offer the safest, highest quality, most reliable, lowest cost blood products in the area. It should also be the leader in supplying safe, low cost, bone products for transplantation.

   Evaluate present program to eliminate problems.

   Evaluate blood production capabilities, local usage and export potential with the production and distribution to exceed 80,000 units.

   Begin an aggressive campaign to educate the community

	with regard to the extensive testing done on ARC donors to alleviate the fear of hepatitis and AIDS.
4. In two years, establish a fully computerized system for monitoring and inventorying whereabouts of ARC blood units between area hospitals.	Use present UPC coding system to inventory as well as follow distribution of blood and tissue products throughout the region.
5. In two years, develop a personal and family blood banking system for the purpose of holding known donations to be given to a particular recipient.	Annual donations of a certain amount would entitle the donor to the opportunity of blood banking to meet a personal or family need.

SECTION VI: Strategic Plan

A. This year:

1. Hold an employee meeting to discuss ideas for increased involvement and planning. Invite a special speaker with expertise in the field of strategic planning to launch this approach.
2. Gradually introduce management by objectives (MBO) to each department of the chapter to increase staff productivity and improve the functioning of the Red Cross as a whole.
3. Establish a monthly schedule for planning sessions with the Board and staff.
4. Assign a task force to develop and refine a two-way communication system between administration and staff.
5. Develop a department for direct mailing and marketing.
6. Write a proposal for a paid staff member to handle special events, grants, and contracts. Determine whether this responsibility can

be assumed by a present employee or whether it should be a new position.

7. Contact an advertising agency with regard to developing commercials and PSA announcements.

8. Establish a task force to develop an application/questionnaire designed to pinpoint specific abilities of volunteers and potential employees.

9. Have computer program written in order to establish a volunteer log in conjunction with the newly developed application.

10. Assign task force of volunteers and staff to analyze the present disaster relief situation.

11. The above task force will accomplish the following tasks:
    a. develop a plan for increasing the volume of relief shelters.
    b. contact potential medical staff to man these shelters.
    c. contact feeding establishments capable of food donations during disaster times.
    d. contact establishments willing to donate clothes and household items.

12. Establish a group to begin working closely with youth agencies (governmental and otherwise) to develop a plan for better coping with increasing juvenile problems such as drug abuse, vandalism, child abuse, etc.

13. Contact various companies with regard to blood drives and tissue services.

14. Further develop existing marketing strategies for bone and tissue programs.

B. Next year:

1. Evaluate the present MBO process to locate deficiencies which need to be eliminated.

2. Develop a volunteer training program in conjunction with a volunteer recognition program.

3. Develop a volunteer recognition program which establishes levels of volunteer achievements to be attained.

4. Campaign in local high schools and youth social clubs to increase youth volunteerism.

5. Assign a building committee including representatives from

the administrative staff and governing board to examine present building requirements and to determine expansion needs.

6. Establish a building fund.
7. Assign a task force to design a plan for improving communication during disaster times.
8. Contact and enlist additional support from the State National Guard. Establish quarterly meetings to discuss increasing social support services.
9. Contact local churches to encourage added support.
10. Begin monthly visitation to schools and colleges to educate students about the work of the ARC.
11. Increase Blood Mobile Unit activity.
12. Contact and develop relationships with area competitors for blood services.
13. Increase blood and tissue service production and distribution to 80,000 units.

C. In two years:

1. Reevaluate and fine tune present MBO systems. Provide a refresher course for departments needing it.
2. Expand educational programs presently being offered. Increase number of volunteer teachers and course locations.
3. Increase number of educational facilities presently being visited by Red Cross volunteers.
4. Further increase Blood Mobile Unit activity.
5. Develop in-home assistance program for the homebound disabled and elderly.
6. Increase collection of food, clothing, etc. from individuals, schools, and other sources.
7. Continue to increase fund raising capabilities independent of those provided by the United Way.
8. Establish a local endowment fund.
9. Develop a cooperative effort between the Red Cross and local social work organizations to meet the needs of local youth.
10. Increase Red Cross visibility in the media through newspaper advertisements and radio and TV announcements.

D. In three years:

1. Reevaluate MBO program.
2. Reevaluate volunteer recognition program. Make adjustments where appropriate and reinstate a drive for new volunteers.
3. Begin campaign for additional funds needed to equip newly acquired disaster shelters.
4. Reevaluate facility utilization and determine if additional space is needed. Further evaluate satellite utilization to determine if additional satellites are needed.
5. Expand public awareness of the safety of ARC blood and tissue products through educational programs and literature.

E. In four years:

1. Invite strategic planning specialist in to determine the effectiveness of the present MBO system.
2. Evaluate progress being made in the area of the endowment fund.
3. Implement computerized blood unit monitoring system for area hospitals.
4. Develop the Personal Blood Banking Program.

SECTION VII: Short-Range Strategic Plan

A. Administrative and Management

1. Schedule a Strategic Planning Seminar for the employees, volunteers, and Board members. Enlist the assistance of a strategic planning specialist to advise and possibly instruct the seminar.
2. Assign a task force to develop and refine a plan for a comprehensive two-way communication system between administration and staff to be implemented by year end.
3. Hold monthly planning sessions with the Board.
4. Increase fund raising capabilities through the development of a direct mailing system and a more comprehensive marketing department.
5. Write a proposal for a paid staff member to handle special events, grants, and contracts.

6. Pursue the development of commercial advertising and PSA announcements.
7. Develop the new volunteer/employee application and have a computer program written to enhance the capabilities of monitoring and logging volunteers and their special abilities.

B. Disaster Services

1. Establish a task force of two staff members and four volunteers for the following:
   a. Disaster–
      1. plot existing disaster shelters on a map.
      2. contact additional places for shelters.
   b. Shelter Staff–contact potential medical personnel to aid at the established shelters during disaster times.
   c. Clothing–contact churches, the Salvation Army, and other establishments to donate clothing, household items, and other needed items for families and individuals during disaster times.
   d. Food–contact feeding establishments to see if they will contribute food during disaster times.
   e. Task Force Structure–
      1. Staff member with two volunteers handle shelter and clothing efforts.
      2. Staff member with two volunteers handle the medical staff and food needs.
2. Assign a task force of two people to work on improvement in communications during times of disaster. These two people can begin with a small "brainstorm" session of what could be done, analyze these ideas and begin developing a communication program. They will report their progress regularly to a board member. Ideas should be implemented as soon as possible.

C. Social Support Services

1. Initiate quarterly meetings with the State National Guard for the purpose of involving them more closely in the activities of the ARC.
2. Contact 50 area churches to enlist increased pledges of financial and other support. Offer educational programs to

train their members to respond appropriately during emergency situations.

3. Target 12 schools and/or colleges to be visited in the next year. Visits should include information about the Red Cross as well as opportunities for students to enroll in courses, donate blood, enlist as volunteers, etc.

4. Increase visits to private corporations by 10 percent a quarter offering similar opportunities listed above.

D. Health and Safety Services

1. Assign a person to construct a list of new courses which need to be developed. By using a source such as the Yellow Pages, target schools where potential instructors can be sought. Keep the list on file for additions and future use.

2. Run monthly ads in local newspaper to announce course offerings and locations. Pursue radio advertisements by considering effectiveness and expense incurred. Also utilize Public Service Announcements.

E. Blood and Tissue Services

1. Assign 2-3 volunteers to send out literature to various companies about blood drives and tissue services. These volunteers will also follow up with phone calls to ensure that literature was received and to inquire as to whether companies would be interested in holding blood drives or learning more about tissue donation.

2. Further develop the existing marketing strategies for bone and tissue programs by doing a small study on recent styles of marketing health care and see which techniques would best serve the ARC's needs.

3. Develop a short questionnaire/survey to determine who donates blood products and with whom they donate. Monitor the community's attitude toward blood services. This survey could be accomplished in several area shopping malls by youth volunteers.

SECTION VIII: *Evaluation and Control*

A. Appraisal

At the end of each fiscal year an evaluation of organizational objectives and goals will be conducted. A chart will be drawn up of the goals and their present status. It will be determined by those involved if the goals were reached, how effectively they were reached, and if these goals were reached efficiently. The overall plan will be reevaluated to strengthen the weak areas and reschedule any incomplete activities.

At a general employee meeting the results will be discussed at length. If the desired results were achieved, recognition of responsible individuals will occur at this time. Outstanding staff members and volunteers will be presented with a framed certificate in honor of a job well done.

If the goals were not met, there will be a discussion as to what was expected, what the actual results were, and what additional work needs to be accomplished. Interaction at this point between the Board and staff members involved is crucial for the continued success of the project. Input and ideas will be noted and included in the revision of the objectives and strategies.

The successful completion of strategic objectives should be noted in the annual evaluation of employees involved. Merit pay increases and promotions should be given in accord with successful strategic planning. The accompanying chart will be used for evaluation and control because it identifies objectives, strategies, timelines and the people responsible for accomplishment of the stated objectives.

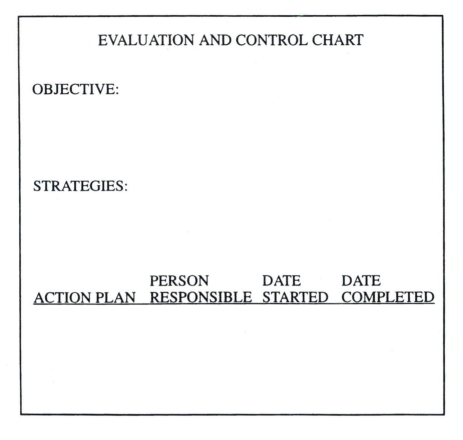

B. Rewards

One of the most important final steps of strategic planning is the establishment of a reward system. For a volunteer organization, such as the Red Cross, it is very important to include the volunteer staff in this reward effort.

During the year, volunteers should be recognized for outstanding achievement and assistance during crisis situations. Small certificates of appreciation and lapel pins noting the number of years (or hours) served should be awarded for specific achievement.

STRATEGIC PLAN FOR A LOCAL CHAPTER
OF THE YOUNG MEN'S CHRISTIAN ASSOCIATION

I. PURPOSE AND MISSION

The purpose of the Metro Young Men's Christian Association (YMCA) is to establish, promote, develop and supervise the work of the Association locally, to wit:

> The improvement of the spiritual, mental, social and physical conditions of all people and to enlist each person in a world-wide fellowship united by common loyalty to the ideals and teachings of Jesus Christ for the purpose of building Christian and religious personality and a Christian and religious society, and to do all other things necessary or which pertain to the proper maintenance, development and extension of the Young Men's Christian Association.

The YMCA is a charitable association dedicated to building healthy experience in mind and body and is part of a worldwide movement. It puts Christian principles into practice through programs that promote good health, strong families, youth leadership, community development, and international understanding. YMCAs are open to men, women and children of all ages, incomes, abilities, races, and religions.

II. ENVIRONMENTAL ANALYSIS

1. The tax-exempt status of not-for-profits is being challenged by private health clubs. YMCA branches in other cities have been accused by private health clubs of not being true community centers and of unfair competition. These cases ended in favor of the YMCA, but private health clubs are carefully monitoring the situation.
2. Americans are increasingly health- and fitness-conscious. According to a Yankelovich Clancy Shulman survey, indications are that Americans in the 90s are more concerned about health than ever before. Also, Americans are developing a more balanced approach to health and fitness rather than the arduous gym regimen of the 80s.

3. There is a larger proportion of aging population. The United States has a sizeable elderly consumer market. It is estimated that there are more than 61 million noninstitutionalized Americans aged 50 and older.

4. There is an increase in program offerings by competitors. Private health clubs are beginning to offer a wider variety of classes and also implementing children's programs rather than focusing strictly on adults.

5. Thirty-four percent of the Metro population is enrolled in a health club. This leaves over 60 percent of the Metro population to be targeted.

6. The number of working mothers has grown substantially in the last thirty years, and is expected to continue to grow along with an increase in both male and female single-parent families in the future.

7. The values, wants, and needs of the Metro population along with many demographic variables, such as population location, age and incomes have changed over the past five years and will continue to change in the future.

8. Industrial and not-for-profit organizations have suffered budget cuts and lowered funding in social programs.

9. There is a decrease in volunteer work and an increase in the demand for more community and social programs.

10. Adults interested in health/fitness programs prefer locations close to their homes, according to a survey done by students at Metro University.

III. STRENGTHS AND WEAKNESSES

1. Strengths
   a. The YMCA has the third largest membership enrollment among local not-for-profit organizations. AAA and AARP are the only other organizations with memberships that exceed the YMCA. Based on this there is obviously a very large following of the YMCA.
   b. The YMCA offers a wide variety of programs and activities.
   c. The YMCA is open to all people regardless of race or financial position. The YMCA makes arrangements with

individuals of lower income who cannot afford regular dues but desire to be a member of the YMCA.

d. The YMCA offers quality services at a competitive price. After comparing the monthly rate of the YMCA with other health clubs in the Metro area it was found that YMCA's monthly dues were competitive.

e. The YMCA has well-established facilities and building sites. The first YMCA building in Metro, the downtown branch, was built in 1913. An organization that has been here for that long and in the same building indicates stability to the community.

f. The overall mission statement is perceived favorably among community members and opinion leaders. Having a mission statement that the community agrees with can bring more support to the organization.

g. The YMCA has a strong volunteer program.

2. Weaknesses

a. The lack of adequate fund-raising campaigns by the Metro area YMCA. The contribution ratio, based on the past year's annual report is 21 percent which is substantially lower than the norm for non-profits which is 64 percent.

b. The lack of an adequate marketing staff and campaign to promote the organization within the community. Currently, the YMCA does not have a main marketing campaign to use in promotion of their services, activities, and facilities.

c. The lack of building sites in key areas creates large areas of unserved markets. Due to the population increase the YMCA does not have adequate facilities to conveniently serve the population in certain locations.

d. Conflicting interests between the different YMCA branches in Metro. Each branch has its own decision making board and budget. Due to this it was found that not much interaction takes place between the different branches. This type of arrangement could cause each branch to have completely different objectives which could cause confusion within the community.

e. Gross expenditures exceeded revenue causing the YMCA

to operate at a deficit. According to the financial statement from the past year's Annual Meeting, the YMCA had a Net Deficiency of $289,658. The Net Operating Ratio shows the excess of revenue over expenditures at –11%.

   f. Programs relating to family support are limited. For example, the YMCA is limited in its ability to offer senior citizen programs. In addition, there is limited cooperation from some public schools for Latch Key programs; limited awareness throughout all branches regarding availability of financial assistance for membership; and a need for more community development.

IV. ASSUMPTIONS

1. The economy will continue to show steady improvement providing the basis for the metropolitan area to achieve steady population growth.
2. The standardized membership fee implemented this year will balance out the use of all facilities and allow Branch Managers to work toward common goals and objectives.
3. The Latch Key program will create greater awareness of the YMCA in areas where the "Y" would like to grow–thus creating a demand and fiscal means for new and improved facilities.
4. The growing fitness trend across America will continue.
5. Not-for-profits will continue to receive their tax-exempt status.
6. The United Way will continue to subsidize approximately 12 percent of the citywide budget.
7. The real estate market will experience a steady increase in the Metro area.

V. OBJECTIVES AND STRATEGIES

1. Objectives

   A. Membership

      1. Increase family memberships by 5 percent next year.
      2. Increase the number of participants in fitness programs by 55 percent over the next two years.

3. Establish monitoring program for YMCA services by the end of next year.
4. Increase membership by 60 percent within the next four years.

B. Program and Participation

1. Plan a fund-raising campaign in the form of a public event to raise approximately $40,000 by end of the summer of next year.
2. In the next two years, establish better access through location, transportation, and communication methods in order to increase program participation by 35 percent.
3. By summer of next year begin competitive sports program at the YMCA among 30 percent of the local churches.
4. Increase program participation by 25 percent for all locations within the next two years.
5. Increase program offerings to senior citizens by 20 percent during the next year.
6. Develop customer satisfaction program by the end of next year.

C. Management and Human Resources

1. Recognition given to outstanding employees on a quarterly basis and special recognition given to Employee of the Year.
2. Implement a goal-setting program and focus group research by the end of next year.
3. Increase volunteer participation through use of such groups as RSVP by the summer of next year.
4. Implement an aggressive marketing campaign within the next two years.
5. Implement a program to increase employee job satisfaction measured by a cultural index tool by next year.

D. Finance

1. Revenue and Expense budget adjusted to accommodate new projects. This will increase operating budget by 35 percent. The ECFA total average operating

ratios (Program Expenses:Total Expenses) shows an average of 80 percent of total expenses go to support charitable programs.

2. Revenue received from internal sources will be used to help eliminate dependance on outside source support by 25 percent. Such support sources include donations from the United Way, and dependency will be reduced by the fall of next year. Last year donations from the United Way amounted to 15 percent of the YMCA's revenue.

3. Increase the endowment fund by 10 percent by working with committee members to improve endowment promotions within the next two years. Last year endowment contributions amounted to only 5 percent of revenue.

4. Develop an annual citywide membership campaign to facilitate membership increases of 20 percent. Last year's membership fees contributed 31.2 percent of revenue.

5. Increase corporate sponsorship by 15 percent within the next year.

2. Strategy

   A. Membership

      1. Mail pamphlets and calendars indicating special programs that will be taking place for each month. This will include members and nonmembers.

      2. Purchase television ad slots showing activities and programs that the YMCA has to offer.

      3. Put on a food fair at river parks with participating local restaurants and food companies.

      4. Put on an olympic sports event where people from all over the city can sign up and pay entry fees to participate in individual and team competition.

      5. Implement a shuttle service between the different YMCA locations.

      6. Implement Elder-Ride and Kids-on-the-Go. Each participant would pay a one-time yearly fee.

7. Increase incentive offerings to include student discounts and senior discounts.
8. Provide "rebates" to existing members or program participants for enrolling new members.

B. Program and Participation

1. Publicize special events in local papers.
2. Distribute flyers to local convenience stores, churches, and schools to make the public aware of the shuttle service.
3. Mail cards indicating the various competitive sports programs that the area YMCAs will be sponsoring.
4. Run membership specials twice a year to increase participation in programs.
5. Sponsor senior citizen trips.
6. Take programs directly into the community.
7. Place suggestion boxes in convenient locations for customer comments and suggestions.

C. Management and Human Resources

1. Create an employee awareness program; an employee will be nominated each quarter for outstanding performance on the job. The individual receiving the award will be selected by his peers.
2. Each area YMCA will select a representative to meet once a month with representatives from other area branches to discuss goals and focus areas.
3. Recruit volunteer local RSVP members to assist with special programs within the YMCA.
4. Hire additional marketing personnel.
5. Implement a volunteer telemarketing program.
6. Increase the use of the media.
7. Develop a corporate culture index to monitor employees' satisfaction.
8. Implement an employee/volunteer-of-the-month award in the form of a plaque, money, or trip.

D. Finance

1. Adjust income and expense reports to reflect increased revenue generated by newly implemented programs.

The ECFA total average operating ratio for support service expense is 20 percent of total expenses.

2. Set aside funding from sources such as the United Way and replace income with newly generated funds. The ECFA total average operating ratio for fund balance reserve is 89 percent of total expenses, and the cash reserve ratio is 15 percent.

3. Endowment Committee will focus attention on new donations.

4. Revenue received from the new membership campaign will be used to improve existing programs. The ECFA total average operating ratio for program expenses is at 80 percent. Last year, Metro YMCA generated 31.2 percent of its revenue from memberships and 40 percent from programs.

5. Aggressively promote the savings to companies through healthier employees from participating in a health maintenance plan.

6. Allow sponsoring companies to use the facilities for conducting recreational activities.

7. Send a monthly newsletter to companies to promote sponsorship and upcoming events.

VI. EVALUATION AND CONTROL

The final step in the plan is to establish the evaluation and control procedures. These procedures provide a means of charting the accomplishment of objectives by identifying responsible parties, timelines, and posting periodic evaluation results. The accompanying chart will be used in the evaluation process and serve as a basis of rewarding people for their efforts in accomplishing objectives. Thus, the reward system is tied to achieving results which have been agreed upon and evaluated.

EVALUATION AND CONTROL CHART

OBJECTIVE:

STRATEGIES:

ACTION PLAN	PERSON RESPONSIBLE	DATE STARTED	DATE COMPLETED

Index